UNRAVELLING CANADA

Sylvia Olsen

Unravelling

CANADA

A Knitting Odyssey

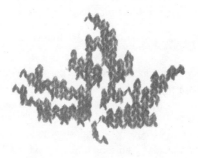

Douglas & McIntyre

*To the handworkers who make beauty, and with
their stories infuse their creations with meaning
and our lives with love and humanity.*

DOUGLAS AND MCINTYRE (2013) LTD.
P.O. Box 219, Madeira Park, BC, VON 2HO
www.douglas-mcintyre.com

EDITED by Audrey McClellan, Barbara Pulling
and Rebecca Pruitt MacKenney
COVER DESIGN by Anna Comfort O'Keeffe
TEXT DESIGN by Shed Simas / Onça Design
PRINTED AND BOUND in Canada
PRINTED ON 100% recycled paper

Canadä Canada Council   Conseil des arts
for the Arts   du Canada   BRITISH COLUMBIA
ARTS COUNCIL   BRITISH
COLUMBIA

DOUGLAS AND MCINTYRE acknowledges the support of the Canada
Council for the Arts, the Government of Canada, and the
Province of British Columbia through the BC Arts Council.

LIBRARY AND ARCHIVES CANADA CATALOGUING IN PUBLICATION
Title: Unravelling Canada : a knitting odyssey / Sylvia Olsen.
Names: Olsen, Sylvia, 1955- author.
Identifiers: Canadiana (print) 20200407392 | Canadiana
   (ebook) 20200407430 | ISBN 9781771622868 (softcover) |
   ISBN 9781771622875 (EPUB)
Subjects: LCSH: Knitting—Canada. | LCSH: Knitting—Social aspects—
   Canada. | LCSH: Knitwear—Canada. | LCSH: Knitwear—Social
   aspects—Canada. | LCSH: Knitters (Persons)—Canada. | CSH:
   Cowichan sweaters.
Classification: LCC TT819.C2 047 2021 | DDC 746.43/20971—dc23

CONTENTS

INTRODUCTION

THE OLD BROTHER KNITTING MACHINE grinds and thuds in protest as Joni, my oldest daughter, pushes it to its limit, feeding heavy raw wool between its slightly too-small needles. She's busy making modern fashions using new machines, new yarns and wool working techniques passed down from her Coast Salish grandmothers. She's creating unique shapes and fabrics to be transformed into bags, pillows, ponchos, skirts and scarfs.

Salish Fusion is our family wool business, located in Tsartlip First Nation (W̱JOȽEȽP), in the territory of the W̱SÁNEĆ people, just north of Victoria, BC. In addition to machine knits, we create knitted things by hand, integrating patterns we love with designs we imagine. Yetsa, my granddaughter, manages our online sales, oversees the website and handles our marketing. The work we produce can also be found in museums, art galleries and craft shows.

Coast Salish woolworkers were innovators. In the early twentieth century they adopted new tools, new materials and new skills from European settlers. Drawing on their age-old talents and practices as blanket weavers and basket makers, they created a knitting method now known as the Cowichan sweater, the only home-grown knitting tradition in North America. At Salish Fusion, we follow this tradition of innovation and honour it to create something unique.

The place where ideas and imagination meet has always interested me. I'm fascinated by the ways humans borrow, share and adapt tools and materials, applying our endless ingenuity, especially as it occurs in the field of handwork. The techniques of Fair Isle knitting from the Shetland Islands, Aran knitting from western Ireland and Guernsey knitting from the islands in the English Channel link and overlap with techniques from Lithuania, Norway and Iceland. That raises questions about how the bright colourwork from Peru, Mexico and Guatemala fits into the global knitting puzzle.

I find questions about whose traditions are whose, who started certain traditions, who owns them and who borrowed them to be deeply personal. Knitting questions lie at the juncture of my English/Scottish/European heritage and my Coast Salish life experiences. My own design work is a fusion, and I cannot unravel one aspect of my life from the other.

Shapes, textures and colour crowd my sleeping mind. When I wake up, I jot my ideas down in graph books or on slips of paper. Eventually I add them to the files on my laptop that I've labelled "Ideas," "Patterns," "Designs" and "Stories."

So far, my designs have been heavily influenced by the thirty-five or so years that I lived in Tsartlip First Nation. I married into the community when I was seventeen and began making wool and knitting soon after. My family ran a business called Mount Newton Indian Sweaters out of a shop behind our house from 1975 to 1991. I spent those years in daily contact with Coast Salish knitters. I bought and sold their knitting to local customers and to several wholesale clients in Banff and Vancouver. I inserted zippers into thousands of sweaters, for my business and for sweater merchants in Victoria and Duncan. I washed, mended, buttoned, pocketed, altered and did pretty much any task that could be performed on something knitted.

The knitters challenged and inspired me to understand knitting through its complexity—design, function, economy, enjoyment, gruelling hard work—and through the simplicity of its beauty.

My designs start with basic shapes that become blank canvases for bands of geometric designs. I am drawn to the symmetry of repetition and am fascinated by how simple symbols have permeated every human culture since we were drawing on the walls of our cave homes. I picture my designs first in undyed natural sheep shades, although colours are edging into my creations.

Over the years, when questions about design and knitting techniques made me think of distant places, my mind kept circling back home. What about Canada? What were Canadians knitting? Was there anything about Canadian knitting that was particularly Canadian? I wanted to know what Canadians were saying about knitting and what knitters were saying about Canada.

Maybe by exploring knitting in my own country I'd find out something about my Canadian identity, I thought. Canada is a huge collection of regions that has been struggling to find an identity since the nineteenth century, when a group of European men stood around a table and decided there should be a federation. The idea of discovering Canadian identity through knitting sounded far-fetched even to me.

But as Albert Einstein said, if an idea does not seem absurd at first, there is no point in pursuing it. I have always been attracted to the places where questions pose a challenge, where the yarn is in a knot. And when I mentioned my idea to Diane Morriss, my publisher for *Knitting Stories*, she offered to organize a cross-country tour for the book. The more we talked, the less absurd the idea became.

I had more than a book tour in mind. I wanted to share my stories about living and working with Coast Salish knitters, but if I was going to search for Canadian identity, I needed to hear stories from other knitters too. The opportunity to conduct workshops across the country was also enticing. All the patterns in *Knitting Stories* contained colourwork, and I was interested in sharing the colourwork technique I use—a technique I had dubbed "Coast Salish colourwork" because Coast Salish knitters used it almost exclusively, and I had acquired it through knitting with Coast Salish women for decades. I was naming something that had never been formally named, creating an identity for the "over/under, never strand even two stitches" technique, and attaching it to a certain group of Indigenous knitters.

Later, as the tour progressed, I began to realize the name was not correct. There was nothing particularly Coast Salish about it, other than the fact that this group had adopted it. Other knitters have also adapted, adopted and amended this colourwork strategy over centuries. It probably dates back as far as knitting itself. There is nothing new under the sun, only variations on a theme. By the time I reached the end of the tour, I had completely rethought the name I had given my workshop at the start. It wasn't just "Coast Salish" colourwork I was teaching, and it was better to think of the technique by its characteristic—it is intuitive. Intuitive Colourwork. I liked how it sounded. It had meaning. A new name emerged.

But those realizations were a few months down the road. As we made final preparations, it became clear that the book tour would be a storytelling tour, as well. It would let me wed my passion for knitting and my obsession with stories. I designed a simple toque to use as a teaching tool. Joni made kits for me to take on the road. Once we posted the news on Facebook, we were committed. The knitting tour was launched.

We set off on April 30, 2015, heading for more than forty knitting destinations, with fifty-two scheduled classes and almost nine hundred participants. Tex McLeod, world traveller and my indomitable partner (now husband), and I packed up our old red Dodge Caravan and set our sights on spending June 15 in Newfoundland.

I hoped to come home with a deeper understanding of knitting, a fresh appreciation for Canada and a renewed sense of being Canadian. Along the road, I intended to find my people.

BRITISH COLUMBIA

FIRST STEPS

SOMETIMES YOU DON'T KNOW HOW to get started with your knitting, and it's not until you knit the first few rounds that your needles fall into place—you get your groove. The knitting tour was a bit like that.

Tex and I had given ourselves six and a half weeks to cross the second-largest country in the world. We initially planned to leave Victoria on May 1. Tex and my publisher, Diane, had worked out the itinerary kilometre by kilometre, hotel by hotel, yarn shop by yarn shop.

It wasn't until mid-April, when I got an email from a neighbour asking where the local workshop was being held, that I realized we hadn't scheduled a workshop at home. Change of plans. Although it seemed slightly off-kilter to start a huge undertaking on the last day of the month, we had no choice. The knitting tour would officially begin on April 30 in Victoria.

We filled my sister Heather's living room that evening with a keen crowd, but I struggled to put my stories into words. I couldn't find my rhythm. I panicked a little, because usually my stories tell themselves; once I start talking, the story lets me know what should be said. Sometimes a story can be obstinate, even impudent, butting into what I am saying and demanding to be told in a different way. But my stories had never let me down.

Telling stories at home was different, I discovered. The act made me self-conscious. I couldn't give my stories a long leash like I usually did, letting them run free to take their own detours and end up in unfamiliar places.

I worried that sisters, children and neighbours would scrutinize what I said at a higher level than strangers did. The people close to any story have versions of their own, and they sometimes dispute the details. That night I pre-thought and rethought what I was saying. In the end my stories weren't any truer, though. They were just hugely overthought and a little clunky. Lesson learned.

With that behind us, we were ready for the next step of the journey. The van was loaded: boxes (and boxes) of knitting kits, boxes (and boxes) of books, our bikes, my current knitting project (a maple-leaf dress—more about that later), clothes, a cooler full of food, cellphones, chargers, and blankets and towels (for a sleep along the road or a spontaneous swim in a lake).

We gave each other a congratulatory, if somewhat apprehensive, high-five as we pulled out of the driveway and headed up Vancouver Island toward Duncan, our original first road-trip destination.

It's only in retrospect that our stop that morning at Tim Hortons in Mill Bay is significant. Every Canadian knows Tim Hortons is the country's quintessential brand. Yet although I like cinnamon raisin bagels and carrot muffins, and once in a while I even enjoy an old-fashioned doughnut hole, I can count on one hand the number of times in a year I make a solo trip to Tim's.

I don't drink coffee. I have never had the inclination. Even the smell of coffee doesn't tempt me. The same cannot be said for Tex. That's why I should have known we would become living proof of the archetypal bumper sticker—the one with the moose crossing the road toward Tim's. It should read: "Tim Hortons, the first stop on every Canadian road trip."

With coffee in hand for Tex and a topped-up water bottle for me, we continued up Highway 1 to Duncan and Cowichan Secondary School. What better place for the first stop on a knitting road trip than a school that shares its name with one of BC's largest First Nations, the Cowichan Tribes, on the home territory of the Hul'qumi'num people, in a town that's at the heart of North America's only knitting tradition? Forty-five years ago, when Cowichan sweaters (or Indian sweaters, as they were commonly called in those days) first became a fascination of mine, the sweaters fuelled a bustling Coast Salish economy.

In those days, Duncan's streets were lined with shops bursting with knitwear. Cowichan sweaters hung in the windows of grocery stores, department stores, gas stations and sporting goods and hardware stores. If you had a retail outlet in Duncan in the 1960s and '70s, chances were you also bought knitting or took it in trade, knowing you could turn a quick dollar selling the famous garments. Walking down the streets of Cowichan Valley communities then, you would see as many Cowichan sweaters as you see fleece jackets today.

That all changed when a convergence of events strangled the Coast Salish knitting industry. In the 1980s, manufactured fibres began to replace heavy wool as the best material for West Coast outdoor garments. By the 1990s, what was once a fashion statement had met the sorry fate of all fashion. Other bulky knits competed with Cowichan sweaters for what was left of the dwindling market.

The decline in the knitting industry did have a good side. Coast Salish women no longer wanted to depend on the pittance they received from the hard work of knitting for a living. They convinced their daughters to stay in school and find work that paid a decent wage.

As far as knitting goes, all was not lost. Knitting reached its nadir in the 1990s and 2000s, but there has been a resurgence in its popularity. While there are no more than a few dozen full-time Coast Salish sweater knitters in the southern part of Vancouver Island now, people are picking up their needles and learning to knit again. They are making small items such as hats and scarfs, but this time for enjoyment, not for employment. The few stores in Duncan that sell First Nations art are filled with woodcarvings, silkscreened clothing, silver jewellery and manufactured items like sunglasses and cellphone covers sporting Indigenous designs. You can still find quality Cowichan sweaters in the small sections set aside for knitting in some stores. You can also find Coast Salish knitters selling their own products online.

While some folks continue to argue about whether the Cowichan people can, or even should, call their sweater Indigenous art, the Cowichan sweater is more than that. It has become an important icon in British Columbia. I maintain that if you want to teach BC history, the Cowichan sweater story tells it all. It's about contact and race relations, power, politics and passion, industry and economy, family, innovation, and survival.

The mystique of the Cowichan sweater comes not only from the creativity and perseverance of the Coast Salish women who made them, or from the interesting fusion of European and Indigenous skills and art, but also from the love and commitment of the people who buy and wear the sweaters. The Coast Salish knitting tradition has found a rightful place in the bigger story of knitting traditions from around the world. The Cowichan sweater is an inspiration. The Cowichan Tribes had to trademark their name to prevent other garment makers from using it, but no one can take away the mythological status their sweaters have acquired. The mythology and the practical reality of knitting, especially Coast Salish knitting, was our knitting tour's raison d'être. With the first workshop at my sister's house under my belt, "Cow High" was the obvious second "first step" on our journey.

The school was holding a professional development day, and seventeen teachers had signed up to spend the morning knitting with me. I caught the first glimpse of something that soon would become obvious: the knitting tour was more than teaching knit and purl stitches. It was bigger than sharing a new way of doing two-stranded colourwork. These were teachers and they were finding the lessons. Some saw the workshop as history—what better way to learn about the Cowichan Valley than the story of the Coast Salish knitters? Others saw it as fashion design, science and innovation, mathematics, or mechanics. They all saw it as a way to teach students how to focus, relax and enjoy the satisfaction of creating something by hand.

ON THE ROAD

IT TURNED OUT THAT GETTING started on our road trip was more like a line dance: "one step forward and two steps back."

Tex is a McLeod—a quintessential Scot—and he knows the value of a dollar. He figured out that we would save the cost of one night at a hotel if we drove back home to Victoria after we finished in Duncan, rather than heading north across the Salish Sea from Nanaimo. That gave us the opportunity the next morning for a third try at the first step of our road trip.

I am about five years old in my first memory of catching the early morning ferry from Victoria to Vancouver. There were seven of us heading to church camp in the Okanagan. My older sister and I argued about who would get to sit in the back of the family station wagon with the suitcases and laundry baskets full of clothes. She won—she always won—but that didn't dampen my wonder at the amber sky and dewy air, or my sizzling anticipation of adventure. My parents were anxiously hoping we'd arrive at the lineup early enough to get on the first ferry of the day. Otherwise it would be a two-hour wait. But I didn't care.

Over the years I would learn that ferry lineups were fun places where islanders met other travellers. Big people kicked tires and talked about how long it would take to get through the mountain passes, while the kids darted in and out of the lines of cars playing tag and hide-and-seek.

I have been both jubilantly the last car to make it onto the ferry and exasperatingly the first car left waiting for the next boat, so my adult rule of thumb is to arrive at least an hour before the ferry sails. I bring my knitting, a book to read and a sketch pad and pencil, and hunker down to enjoy the wait.

Having a love of both early mornings and ferry lineups, I was ready to go by 5:30 a.m. Tex, a newcomer to the island, went along with the plan, but he failed to appreciate my enthusiasm.

Once we were on board, we braved the lineup for the famous BC Ferries breakfast buffet, served in a restaurant that sits high over the bow and boasts a 180-degree view no matter where you sit. Muted morning shades of grey and lavender coloured the layers of mountains disappearing into the distance. The ferry cut a frothy white collar into the glassy cobalt sea. I took a deep breath to catch a hint of the salty, seaweed scent of my favourite scene and laughed. Tex had already settled into a chair with eggs, bacon, fried tomatoes, dim sum, stewed strawberries, orange juice, toast and coffee. Breakfast smells would have to do for now.

Later we went up onto the deck, Tex in search of leaping orcas, me to breathe in the last of the West Coast.

"Let the Great Canadian Knitting Tour begin," Tex said as we drove down the ferry ramp at the Tsawwassen terminal, headed for Vancouver.

"The name sounds presumptuous, almost embarrassing," I said, a bit worried.

"Maybe so, but who else has done something like this? And until they do, this *is* the Great Canadian Knitting Tour."

Diane had had more requests than we could fit into the two days scheduled for Vancouver. More than eighty knitters had booked into four workshops, two groups at the Vancouver Guild of Fibre Arts and two at Wet Coast Wools. As the first room filled up, I got a glimpse of the amazing wealth of knitting experience I was about to encounter. Two of my workshop goals, to tell knitting stories and to demonstrate my favourite colourwork technique, were going to be easy. I quickly realized my third goal, to listen to everyone else's knitting stories, was the challenge—there would simply not be time.

I delivered the message early. "I would love to do nothing but listen to your stories. But if stories are like icebergs, we only have time for the tips. The rest of the story, unfortunately, must be left underwater."

Thankfully, most people complied. And to my surprise, the tour was quickly becoming a show-and-tell event. Women arrived dragging bags containing their old sweaters for me to examine. Some had read the Facebook request I had posted saying that I was looking for the oldest sweater in the country. Others, who had heard I was a knitting historian, simply wanted me to piece together the stories of their sweaters.

WHAT'S REAL?

A WOMAN DRESSED WITH CASUAL elegance set a bag on the table and pulled out what she called her favourite sweater.

"Is this real?" she asked me. "I always wanted a real Cowichan sweater, so I bought this one at a second-hand store years ago. I didn't like the zipper, so I took it out and crocheted on a button band. Then I added extra to the collar so I could button it around my neck. I also knit the pockets and sewed them on the front. I know the wool doesn't match exactly, but I think it works."

Everyone crowded around for an up-close examination. The sweater was white, black and grey with a bluish tinge— close, but not quite the right colours for a Cowichan sweater. Her sweater was old, but the yarn still hadn't faded. There was no question: the wool had been commercially dyed. Pulling apart a loose end, I determined unquestionably that the wool was six-stranded White Buffalo–type yarn, tightly twisted as if done by an Indian Head spinner (a spinner with a large head invented by Coast Salish people to accommodate the bulky yarn they used in their sweaters).

"At a glance, I would say no, it's not a 'real' Cowichan, because one of the hallmarks of Coast Salish knitting is its use of undyed local sheep's wool," I told her. "But then again, I remember people giving Laura, my mother-in-law, White Buffalo wool they didn't want. Its fine strands fell apart in your hands, but she ran it through her spinner and was delighted with the outcome. She didn't care that the wool was

11

dyed. She knit many sweaters that looked very much like this one. So you tell me," I said to the group. "Does it mean it wasn't a Cowichan because she made it with commercial, store-bought, dyed wool? Or was every sweater Laura knit, even if it had cables and plain colours, a Cowichan or Coast Salish sweater because she was Coast Salish?"

The woman's sweater had drop sleeves like a Cowichan. It had intuitive colourwork like a Cowichan. It had a knit-on collar like a Cowichan. It had an exposed three-needle cast-off on the shoulders like a Cowichan. It had geometric designs placed in three white and black bands with a grey background like a Cowichan.

"This is either a Cowichan look-alike made by a knitter who copied all the construction techniques," I said, "or it is a Cowichan made by a knitter who was not constrained by the current rules of authenticity—one who used whatever yarn she wanted to make her sweater. I'm leaning toward the second explanation, because very few knitters who copied Cowichan sweaters in the '70s knit them this well. And then you added your own style to the sweater with the button band, collar and pockets, which makes it even more authentic. You have followed the tradition of innovation."

GENUINE

ONE OF MY WORKSHOP GOALS was to answer some of the simple questions people have about Cowichan sweaters. One of those questions is why the sweaters are called Cowichan and the knitters are called Coast Salish. Here's the reason. Coast Salish people who lived in villages such as T'Sou-ke, Esquimalt, Tsartlip, Tsawout, Malahat, Cowichan, Stz'uminus and Snaw-naw-as on southern Vancouver Island began knitting what are now called Cowichan sweaters sometime before 1920. The sweaters were not a Cowichan invention, nor did they necessarily originate with the Cowichan Tribes. Cowichan is only one of the Coast Salish tribes, but it is the largest, and since their nation is situated in the centre of the knitting region, it didn't take long for the sweaters to become known by their name.

In every place we visited, people brought a wide variety of bulky-knit sweaters, from Mary Maxim and curling and bowling sweaters to home and commercially hand-knit White Buffalo sweaters. They brought hand-knit Icelandic, Aran, Fair Isle and Cowichan sweaters. They wanted to know if their sweaters were genuine—if they were what they were said to be—and if they were authentic—could I tell them about the sweaters' origins?

My challenge was to trace the roots of each sweater, imagining the time period and the knitter through an analysis of the yarn, construction details and design. To some this might seem like an insignificant inquiry, but to me and to the other knitters it was a way of exploring connections to family and heritage and to the history of our country. In addition, it helped me find answers to some of the questions about shared techniques and cultural appropriation that I had been asking for years.

Is it cultural appropriation to teach a knitting technique used for years by knitters across the globe that also happens to be the one most commonly used by Coast Salish knitters? The question is as absurd as asking if knitting bulky sweaters with designs is cultural appropriation. But is it cultural appropriation to copy a specific design or to copy the general look of Cowichan, Icelandic, Fair Isle or Aran sweaters? They are all unique knitted creations from small identifiable regions that have become widely beloved and have provided inspiration to knitters across the globe.

The question of appropriation is important. For example, I believe it is utterly inappropriate for people with no connection to a culture to use significant forms of ceremonial identification, such as feathered headdresses and face paint, for their own purposes. This behaviour goes beyond poor form and insensitivity. It transgresses an honoured social agreement as important as respect for the elderly and care for children. Some behaviour is just wrong.

I also believe we can take the argument of cultural appropriation into areas where it doesn't belong. For example, a friend asked me one day if it was okay for her to wear her Cowichan poncho, or if I thought it was cultural appropriation. She had been on a camping trip with a local elected official, and he had asked her to take it off. "You aren't wearing that when I'm around," the official had said. "It's cultural appropriation."

This is an example of letting our sentimentality get in the way of good thinking. Knitting was not traditional. Knitted clothing was not used ceremonially. Except in the early years, Coast Salish women did not usually knit sweaters for their families to wear. They knit clothing to sell. Knitting was business, a primary source of income for Coast Salish people in the mid- to late twentieth century. Coast Salish women borrowed knitting techniques and tools from the Europeans and created a uniquely identifiable sweater that people bought by the thousands. Coast Salish knitters made Cowichan sweaters. The people who bought them and wore them and cherished them made the sweaters famous. The knitters were knitting as an economic venture. And, lucky for them, in spite of the hard work, they loved what they did. Many Coast Salish knitters told me over the years, "I love the idea that people will wear my sweaters and enjoy them."

To cast a false protectionism over Indigenous women is to deny their roles as businesswomen and caretakers of their families. Reducing Coast Salish knitting to a tradition relegates Indigenous women to the past and diminishes their achievement of transitioning their handworking skills into the future.

The real crime against Coast Salish knitters and the Cowichan sweater is false representation: non-Indigenous companies creating Cowichan-like sweaters and marketing them as Cowichan, Indian, West Coast or similar brand names in an effort to mislead customers into buying their knock-offs.

In the past, Coast Salish knitters cried foul not only because of cultural appropriation, but because these unfair business practices cut into their incomes. They also cried foul because false claims and stolen identities offend what is genuine and authentic, and these are characteristics we value as human beings. Regarding appropriation, many Coast Salish knitters would have the same response my daughter Joni had when she heard about the official who had reprimanded my friend. "What does he think he is doing? That is not good for business."

Fortunately, the heated days of competition and blatant misrepresentation by companies producing counterfeit sweaters has cooled down. These days Cowichan sweaters occupy a unique place in the market. Other bulky sweaters with colourful designs continue to be sold, though Cowichan Tribes controls the use of its name to ensure their sweaters are not misrepresented. Bands of design interspersed with bands of plain colour, natural undyed yarn and the warm inviting bulkiness of these sweaters speak for themselves and will always say "Cowichan."

The art of knitting has been borrowed and shared for hundreds of years. It cannot be called traditional by anyone, including Europeans or even North Africans, where knitting appears to have started. In the same way Coast Salish knitters used techniques from Europe to make their sweaters, knitters from across the globe have incorporated Coast Salish techniques into their designs, and the wonderful cycle of creativity goes on. These days it is often hard to distinguish between Coast Salish, Guatemalan, Peruvian and Ecuadorian knitting. The important thing about authenticity is to call a spade a spade. Acknowledge where you get your inspiration, and then enjoy this unique cross-cultural fusion called knitting.

I told the woman in Vancouver with the confusing sweater, "I know you would prefer an 'either it is or it ain't' explanation. But your sweater is more interesting than that. It is a fusion. I think there is something genuinely Canadian about that."

On my knitting tour I found out that identities and names are as confusing and changeable as they are important. As I said earlier, knitters who make Cowichan sweaters are not necessarily Cowichan people; they are also people from neighbouring First Nations. Cowichan people, like Indigenous people across Canada, are increasingly calling themselves by their own name, Hul'qumi'num, meaning "warmed by the sun." People from Saanich are now W̱SÁNEĆ, which means "emerging land"; people from Victoria are Ləkʷəŋən, "the place where herring fish are smoked"; and people from Nanaimo are now Snuneymuxw, "great people."

Remembering and using names is an important part of getting to know the new and emerging Canada as it becomes aware of its histories. If I took another Canadian road trip, I would think more deeply about the Indigenous names and meanings of the places I visited. For now I use the common Canadian names, which often have to do with names of settlers and foreign histories.

Many Canadian names, however, are anglicized versions of Indigenous words. Take "Canada," for instance. The name first appeared on a map of the world in 1547. The story is that French explorer Jacques Cartier learned the name *kanata*, meaning "village" or "settlement," from Chief Donnacona's sons during his sixteenth-century visit to Stadacona on the St. Lawrence River. By the eighteenth century the whole region along the Great Lakes, now part of Ontario, was called Upper Canada, and the region along the St. Lawrence out to the Atlantic became known as Lower Canada. In 1867, when the Fathers of Confederation discussed naming the new nation, they brought other names to the table such as Britannia, Cabotia and Victorialand, after Queen Victoria. I am thankful that after much discussion they discarded the blatantly European titles and settled on a word with Indigenous connections . . . Canada. There is something Canadian about their decision.

I would also learn on my knitting road trip that knitters honestly want to use the right words and do the right thing. I think there is something Canadian about that as well.

Cowichanesque

DURING MY SIX WEEKS ON the road, I had the privilege of listening to something like eight hundred stories from the knitters who attended the workshops. I knew this book would not be complete without including some of their thoughts, their ideas and their stories—about knitting, about Canada, about Canadian knitting.

I KNIT A COWICHAN-TYPE SWEATER for myself when I was in university. I'm pretty sure I just called it a Cowichan sweater. I didn't know the difference. In fact, I remember thinking I was somehow honouring the real sweaters by calling my sweater Cowichan. It seemed like the right thing to do at the time. A visiting Japanese couple saw it and offered to buy it. I couldn't believe anyone would buy my knitting right off my back. But I needed the money, so I sold it. They came back later and asked me to knit another one that was smaller. They wanted more, but two was enough for me. That was the end of my knitting career.

A TREASURE

UNTIL WE SET OFF ON our road trip, the oldest sweater I knew about was one I had acquired from Skip Crawford of Saanichton. Skip lived just a few minutes from my house. His uncle Reg had been the dentist in the community in the 1920s and '30s and had bought the sweater from a knitter from Tsawout First Nation—the First Nation neighbour closest to my home in Tsartlip. Skip remembers his uncle wearing the sweater all the time until he died in 1951. He then left it to his nephew. Skip estimated that the sweater must have been knit in the first few years of the 1930s.

Skip wore the sweater for many years, until he became too big for it. After that he stored it in the closet. He brought it over to my place when he heard that I studied old sweaters. He was willing to give it to me for free, but once I saw it I knew I needed to give him something for it. I knit him a new vest in exchange.

Skip's uncle's sweater is an exceptional example of Coast Salish knitting from a time when knitters were free to be creative, before their sweaters became commercialized and had to conform to a set standard of authenticity, which effectively labelled dyed, processed yarn and intricate stitch-work as inauthentic. The main body of Skip's sweater was knit with unprocessed handspun yarn, but it included highlights of bright orange cotton yarn at the ribbing and the cuffs. Surprisingly, the sweater also has ladders of moss stitch, something you won't find in newer sweaters. It's an interesting glimpse into the world of Coast Salish knitters when they were experimenting with different knitting techniques and uses of materials and colour—before what Laura, my mother-in-law, described as "the time when they told us what to knit."

A MEXICAN SWEATER

TEX AND I PLANNED TO pace ourselves during our road trip, taking breaks from knitting and teaching to walk, bike, read and experience the cities we were visiting. After our workshop at Wet Coast Wool in Vancouver, we headed up the road for a stroll. The neighbourhood we were in, Kitsilano or Kits, is known for grand old houses, though the 1920s and '30s architecture now often serves as a façade for converted condominiums. Kits is a place where hipsters, academics, enviros and West Coast groovies enjoy perennial gardens and moss-covered rockeries. The neighbourhood is like a tree emporium. Chestnuts, weeping willows, flowering cherries, elms and catalpas control traffic, shade moms and dads pushing designer baby buggies and turn the heads of amblers upward in pure enjoyment.

"Earrings. A good pair of shoes. A beautiful linen tablecloth."

On the corner stood an elderly woman calling out her wares in a thick Eastern European accent. When she saw my eyes dart straight to the folded sweater in the centre of her blanket, she said, "It's a Mexican sweater. A beautiful Mexican sweater."

"It's a Cowichan sweater," I said.

"A Mexican sweater."

"No, this sweater was made on Vancouver Island. It's a very famous sort of sweater called Cowichan."

"Twenty-five dollars. Yeah? It's a good Mexican sweater."

"Yes. Yes. It's a good sweater."

Tex was already pulling the money from his wallet.

"Thank you. Thank you. Thank you."

It would be an interesting addition to my sweater collection. Its fine-spun, tight knit and intricate eagle design were the work of a skilled knitter. The signature collar was expertly attached—this knitter had made many, many such sweaters. I couldn't tell for sure, but the texture of the wool made me think it was hand carded. The main colour had faded from grey to brown. While the white had once been very white, it had yellowed with age.

Tex asked me, "How old?"

"Maybe the 1970s or early '80s. It's a bomber, and those were pretty popular in those days. Maybe even as early as the mid-'60s, but probably not. I'm thinking it's somewhere between thirty-five and fifty years old."

The sweater's tight rib and short length would have suited me perfectly in an earlier era. I would have worn it with a curly perm and high-waisted pocketless jeans.

"You like the Mexican sweater, yeah?"

"Yes. Thank you. I love it."

FOR REAL

MY PERSONAL SEARCH FOR WHAT it means to be genuine goes back to when I first got to know my mother-in-law, Laura Olsen. She was a Coast Salish woman who lived until she was ninety-three. Laura learned to knit as a little girl, during school breaks, but she had been knitting pretty much full-time since she got out of residential school at the age of fifteen. During the seventy-eight years that followed, she said she knit on average more than ten sweaters a year. That means she knit somewhere around a thousand sweaters in her lifetime. She couldn't have counted how many hats, slippers and mittens she had knit. Right from the start, Laura and I made wool together, and she encouraged me to knit. She told me to copy the sweaters I liked. She said that's how the Coast Salish learned to knit in the first place.

"We pulled old sweaters apart, ones we got second-hand. We figured out how they were knit, and we copied them stitch for stitch. Then we made changes and put our own personal style onto the sweaters."

Laura didn't like making "Cowichan sweaters" in the formal sense. She didn't like being constrained by someone else's ideas of authenticity or genuineness. She embodied genuine. She made what she liked, and she liked what she made: Laura originals.

"Pretty soon," she told me, "you'll get your own style."

In the end, the wool I spun felt a lot like her handspun. Some of her favourite designs are my favourite designs, and some of the sweaters I knit resemble hers. As she promised, I have developed a style of my own, one that keeps evolving but is deeply rooted in the place where it all started—sitting next to Laura making wool. She said my daughters would probably knit like I did, which meant in some small way they would knit like she had. I was the bridge and she was happy about that.

Boyfriend Sweaters

BOYS BUY GIRLS RINGS. WE knit them sweaters. The sweater often becomes the barometer, the stitch gauge and the stitch count for the relationship.

I STARTED KNITTING MY BOYFRIEND a sweater and only got just past the ribbing before we split up. I was so mad at him I chucked the whole thing, yarn and all, in the garbage.

MY BOYFRIEND ALWAYS WORE SWEATERS, and I imagined that if I made him one, it would be his favourite. You know, the one he put on all the time, the one that made him think of me. I admit the sweater didn't turn out quite as great as I hoped. The shape was a bit strange. He wore it a few times to make me happy, and then the sweater sort of disappeared. So much for that relationship.

I WORKED SO HARD ON making my boyfriend a sweater. It was the first and only knitting I had ever done. I wanted it to be a surprise for him. It was almost finished when he dumped me. I ripped it out. Every stitch. I intended to knit something else with the wool but lost my interest in knitting after that. Eventually I sent the balls of yarn to the second-hand store.

⸙

I WANTED TO KNIT MY boyfriend a big, bulky, cuddly sweater, sort of like my arms around him all the time. I don't know what I was thinking while I was knitting—why I didn't see it coming. When I was finished, it was like he was wearing a tent. The sleeves came down to his knees. When I tried to shrink the sweater, it felt like cardboard.

⸙

I SHOULD HAVE KNOWN THE relationship wasn't going to work. I started knitting a sweater for my boyfriend about a dozen times. Each time was a different sort of disaster. I couldn't get it right. I pulled it back so often the yarn started to fray. In the end, it never did fit him right or look any good. I don't know if he ever wore it.

⸙

MY HUSBAND SAW AN AD in the paper about a knitting class. He thought it would be a good place to meet women. He was right. I was there. I learned to knit. He didn't. We got married, and I'm still knitting for him thirty-five years later.

TEX'S SWEATER

"IN MY YOUNGER DAYS, WHEN I lived on a commune in northern Ontario, a woman told me she wanted to knit me a sweater," Tex said as we strolled along.

"A sweater?" This surprised me. He had never mentioned it before.

"She asked me what colour I wanted," he said. "'What colour? How about you pick the colour?' I told her.

"'No. No,' she said. 'I want it to be your favourite colour.'

"'Green, then.'

"We never even got together. Well, maybe one night or so. I still have that sweater. It's a bright green turtleneck, Saskatchewan Roughrider green. It's frayed now and has holes in it. That was forty-five years ago. I don't know. Maybe she knit all the guys sweaters."

THE OTHER DAY, TEX PULLED the sweater out of his closet and put it on. The Saskatchewan Roughrider green had faded to more insipid shades in several places, and moths had munched holes all over.

"I could wear this. It still fits," he said, standing tall. "What do you think?"

"I think it's had better days, but it makes me wonder about the 'one night or so.'"

I wondered how the woman would tell the story of the green sweater.

THE ROAD

WE PULLED OUT OF VANCOUVER at seven o'clock the next morning, and within thirty minutes the concrete and tall buildings were behind us. We headed down Highway 1, anticipating about five hours to our next destination, the Okanagan.

Tex held the steering wheel with his left hand while his right hand fiddled with the radio volume. I had set my knitting basket on the floor of the passenger's side. My design graph was folded on the console, and my legs were stretched out so my feet could rest on the dash. About three inches of my Canadian-knitting-tour red-maple-leaf dress sat on my lap. As the Fraser Valley whizzed by on either side, we found ourselves face to face with majestic Mount Baker ascending out of a sea of mist into the blue sky. I was in bliss.

The Trans-Canada Highway, our chosen path, is the longest national highway in the world and also the shortest route across the country. If you are in a hurry, hypothetically you can get from one end of the 7,821-kilometre highway to the other in just over three days, excluding the ferries on the West and East Coasts.

Brigadier Alex Macfarlane is famously said to have taken nine days in 1946 to make the maiden Canadian motor crossing, driving from Louisbourg, Nova Scotia, to Victoria (Newfoundland was not yet a province of Canada). That was four years before the first crew set out to pave a road across the country. In 1962, Prime Minister John Diefenbaker celebrated the completion of the Trans-Canada Highway, but it would be eight more years before the last gravel sections were paved.

Road trips are about choices, and in general I had left the decisions about destinations to Diane, who set up the workshops, and the decisions about travel details to Tex, who arranged our route and accommodations. But I had a few personal requests—places I didn't want to miss. Ever since my first road trip as a kid to the Okanagan, old friends and nostalgia have kept drawing me back.

I always anxiously await the steep mountain passes along the Fraser Canyon, where the river plunges through the Coast Range. In the early 1960s there were barely two lanes of road. We would pass crews blasting tunnels through giant granite outcroppings and wait our turn at detour signs that sent cars across temporary single-lane trestles. Thankfully, tunnels and hefty protective barriers now shield travellers from the terrifying view, and I no longer need to bury my face in my sleeve as the road winds higher and higher.

I still breathe a sigh of relief when the landscape calms down east of Lytton and the arid landscape strips the air of its mountain richness. As a child I was in awe of the wide-open sky and the waves of wind rolling through the golden fields of long grass. I dreamed of stripping naked and lying on my back to bathe in them. Then as now I kept my eyes peeled for a glimpse of a real live cowboy.

Tex and I found A Twist of Yarn, Vernon's only wool shop, in an old Victorian-style house on a residential street. When we opened the front door, two young girls came running down the stairs from their family apartment on the top floor. Their mom, Camella, followed them, and later their dad, Ryan. The family greeted us with hugs as if we had been invited for dinner. Although what had been the dining room and living room of the old house were now lined with balls of yarn and racks of needles, the intimacy of home was palpable.

Camella had arranged to host two workshops at a friend's house on the beach at Okanagan Lake. A wall of windows framed the ochre evening light that glinted off the boiling charcoal water. Willows snapped against the glass as a spring storm brewed. It was the kind of night I had faced with a mixture of fear and excitement as a child when my family camped at the lake. We would wrap ourselves in our sleeping bags and hunker down, hoping not to get blown away.

Some women came to the workshops in pairs, but it wasn't long before almost everyone had something in common—a connection with their knitting home. At A Twist of Yarn I recognized the same camaraderie I had witnessed at Wet Coast Wools. I didn't yet fully comprehend the phenomenon of yarn shops, but I was beginning to realize there was something pretty special going on.

ALTHOUGH ART OF YARN IN Kelowna, just forty-five minutes from Vernon, was located in a strip mall on a main street, the shop had the same coming-home feel. Going into the shop, with its wall-to-wall, ceiling-to-floor yarn, felt like climbing into a sweater.

Mothers came to my workshops with their daughters, and friends came with friends. The average workshop attendee so far had been middle-aged, but there was already evidence of a growing trend. Younger knitters are upending one of the many myths about knitters—that knitting is for grandmothers. The yarn selection in the shops I had visited to date conveyed the sense that the knitting scene had found a new groove. Conventional thinking is that grandmothers buy inexpensive, synthetic yarns to knit baby garments, yet in these shops I hadn't seen any of the formerly ubiquitous pink, blue and yellow acrylics. Instead the stacks were filled with unique artisan yarns, perfect for fashionable designs that would appeal to sophisticated, fashion-conscious people, old and young alike.

Armstrong was our next stop. When we arrived at the address we had for the yarn shop, we discovered it was a sparsely furnished room in a row of old buildings on the main street. The owner, Kathleen, had cut a door from her women's clothing store through to her new business venture, The Twisted Purl Yarn Studio. The floors had newly laid hardwood, and the yarn cubbyholes were beautifully shaped coves lined with Douglas fir. The shop itself was an emerging work of art.

At that time Kathleen had not yet built her clientele, but she was working on the premise that if you build a welcoming space and fill it with beautiful yarn, the knitters will come. Six or seven of her excited supporters attended the workshop, and they all shared her confidence. When I asked them if Armstrong, a town of fewer than five thousand people, was big enough to support a yarn shop, they expressed their conviction that the city's heart and enthusiasm would more than make up for its lack of population.

MY CANADIAN DRESS

IT WENT WITHOUT SAYING THAT if I was going on a cross-country knitting road trip, I was going to knit a Canadian dress. Before we left home I drew several maple-leaf motifs. I chose the one I liked best and then intertwined it, Escher-like, on a large graph. I bought red, medium grey, light grey and charcoal Cascade 220 and a 5 mm circular needle. I was ready for my maple-leaf dress to emerge.

By the time we left Kelowna en route to Armstrong, I was already having doubts. I examined what was becoming a predominantly red dress. Given the sharp-edged maple leaf I was using, it was beginning to look like I would be wearing a stylized Canadian flag, and that wasn't working for me.

I have an ambivalent relationship with my country. Like most Canadians, I think Canada is the best country in the world. Even the United Nations has ranked Canada among the top ten countries globally in terms of human development. But I'd lived most of my adult life on a First Nations reserve where poverty, discrimination and desperate living conditions abound. When the UN assesses the situation of First Nations in Canada, the country's rating plummets as low as sixty-third on the world scale. We stubbornly refuse to settle the legal Indigenous land disputes that trouble every region of the country. Canada is also becoming a laggard internationally in the field of environmental protection. Oh, the list of what Canada could do better is long.

Wearing a red maple leaf also felt too much like wearing a political colour. If I was going to wear a colour to match my politics, it would have to be green.

I pulled out my needle and started to tear the dress back.

"What the hell are you doing?" Tex exclaimed.

"Dramatic design change," I told him.

"You've got at least six inches knit already. You could just start again and use that for something else."

It was the Scottish thing again. Tex doesn't like waste, and obviously that extended to stitches.

"But I don't want it for anything else."

"That pulling-stuff-out thing is for the birds," he appealed. "Why don't you turn it into a scarf or placemats?"

A scarf or placemats? Really, Tex?

"We need to stop at Camella's again on the way through. I'm going to buy green yarn to replace the red."

"Green maple leaves?"

Tex has no ambivalence about his country. His Scottish grandparents settled in the Ottawa Valley. He was born and raised in Oakville. He homesteaded in Maple Leaf, near Algonquin Park in central Ontario. He lived in Toronto. He has property in Muskoka. He reads the *The Globe and Mail* and listens to CBC. His favourite artists are the Group of Seven, he cheers for the Toronto Maple Leafs and he loves Neil Young's music. A friend calls him the Canadian Shield. If Canada is looking for a poster boy for Canadian identity, Tex would be a good candidate. He thought tearing out red maple leaves to replace them with green was wrong on many counts.

Notwithstanding his objections, by the time we reached A Twist of Yarn I was happily ready to start again. The red yarn was neatly re-balled and stored for another project. I bought four skeins of bright-green Cascade 220 from Camella to contrast with the greys I was using for background. I could see my new dress already: a bevy of green maple leaves, strikingly Canadian, very West Coast and perfectly Sylvia.

Connections?

AFTER HEARING ALL YOUR STORIES about the sweaters you knit for your boyfriends and husbands, I'm going straight home after this class and asking my husband once and for all where he got his White Buffalo sweater. I can tell it was hand-knit, because it wasn't done very well. The seams are big and bulky, and the collar is sort of lopsided. The sweater has stretched all out of shape, and the cuffs are frayed. I can even see a couple of mistakes in the snowflake design, which has always bugged me. But every time we go out, what does he put on? That disgusting old sweater. I literally have to pull it off his back and force him to wear something else. I thought he just had really bad taste, until today. Now I'm thinking that old rag must have been knit by a former girlfriend. Maybe it's not the sweater he's attached to. Maybe it's the memories. Maybe it's her.

HUNDREDS OF KILOMETRES LATER . . .

THE FIRST SWEATER I KNIT was for my boyfriend. He wanted one of those bulky White Buffalo sweaters. I didn't even know how to knit, never mind starting with such a complicated pattern. I had to figure it out as I went along. I was pretty embarrassed by the time I was finished. There were so many mistakes in it. The snowflake design was really messed up, but I didn't want to pull it back. I did

36

a really bad job of sewing the seams up, and the collar was a mess. The sweater was miles too big for him. But he loved it. He wore it everywhere. I heard he wore it for years, even after we broke up. I've lost track of him now.

BORDERS

WHEN WE LEFT ARMSTRONG, WE had a four-and-a-half-hour drive to reach Winlaw, in the Slocan Valley, the home of my publisher for several books, Sono Nis Press. I knew Diane had dinner and guests waiting.

"I'm excited to drive through the Rockies," I said to Tex.

"We won't see the Rockies until we leave the Kootenays," he said. "We have to pass through the Monashee, Selkirk and Purcell ranges first. The Rockies are only a narrow strip of mountains right on the Alberta border."

I was beginning to realize how little I knew about my home province. Driving through the mountains, there is no telling one range from the next.

I put my knitting down. The maple-leaf design on my dress was too hard to follow with my head bobbing left and right. It felt as if we were driving through postcard locations: sparkling lakes, winding rivers in peaceful valleys, snow-capped mountains. The landscape looked surreal, as if it were staged for a photo shoot, except for the houses. Fences and gardens and bicycles leaning up against sheds and barns reminded me that these were places people lived in and loved. I tried to imagine calling them home.

Lines on a map try to impose political order onto Canada. Borders reflect a ten-mile-high view of the country, and in that sense I have always been British Columbian first and Canadian second. My province feels like the younger sister occupying the space on the other side of the Great Divide. Tex is Canadian first, Ontarian second.

"It's the same thing," he says. "Ontario *is* Canada."

Therein lies one of our country's identity issues. The assumption by central Canadians that they represent the real Canada doesn't sit so easily with those of us who hail from places that have never been the home of an elected prime minister and never won the NHL Stanley Cup. Even British Columbia's Emily Carr, whose art rivalled that of Lawren Harris, A.Y. Jackson and the others, was never accepted by Canada's art crowd in the same way as the Group of Seven.

I thought about it. Did I even feel British Columbian first, or was I first from the Saanich Peninsula? Did other British Columbians see themselves as being first from the Cowichan Valley, the Okanagan or the Chilcotin—places that aren't defined by lines on most maps? Many of the place names in the province are Indigenous, suggesting a different method of demarcating boundaries. Mountain ranges, straits, river valleys and various ecosystems map out Indigenous peoples' territories organically, each with its own history.

Tex and I were heading to the Kootenay region, home to the people of the Ktunaxa Nation. The Kootenays are British Columbia's portion of the Columbia River Basin, providing residents with abundant natural resources and strikingly beautiful places to live and play. This was where several waves of immigrants, including Doukhobors, Mormons and US draft evaders, settled when they were looking for an escape from church, state or war. Each group sought to recreate society around ideas of home-grown self-sufficiency. The Kootenays were also one of the places the federal government chose to intern Japanese citizens during World War II.

Did the area's majestic ecosystems absorb these lived experiences to produce the unique inhabitants of this mountain place? There is no confusing the residents of the Kootenays, with their roots in social protest, with the people of the Okanagan, who appear predominantly business-oriented, seeking success and fun. You can see the difference in the slower way Kootenay women walk and the lighter cadence of their voices. Time is etched more softly on their faces. No one has rushed through traffic in the Kootenays to get where they are going.

One of my workshops was held in a feminine version of a rugby clubhouse, a refurbished one-room schoolhouse that the crafters of the tiny hamlet of Winlaw had bought collectively and made their own. The well-hidden treasure sat just off the main highway in a meadow only steps from the Slocan River. The room was a storytellers' haven. The walls had heard stories before, and the building seemed to have endless time to listen.

We met another group of area knitters at Maplerose, a combination art store and yarn shop a few kilometres up the road in downtown Nelson. The group crowded onto benches in the corner of the shop while customers came and went, some lingering around the edges of our gathering long enough to hear the stories.

In a sense I was home—Sono Nis Press has carved out its place in the forest overlooking the Slocan Valley. Diane and I spent a day winding and weighing balls of wool for the workshop knitting kits and refilling boxes with books. She also downloaded some audiobooks onto Tex's iPhone so we could listen to stories on the road.

I left my province wondering about the stereotype of granola-eating, environment-defending, van-driving, bud-smoking British Columbians. Tex and I decided that if you added Cowichan sweater–wearing to the potpourri of laid-back pastimes, at least then there would be an element of truth in the stereotype.

I had met two types of knitters so far: those who had owned and proudly worn Cowichan-type sweaters and those who had wanted to. I was starting to understand that British Columbians didn't just love Cowichan sweaters; they loved every facsimile of them too. Whether they were reminiscing about bygone days, when being cool meant wearing a Cowichan and driving a Volkswagen van, or were expressing interest in the sweater's association with First Nations culture, the knitters we met confirmed how central the Cowichan sweater is to the province's image. Bulky wool sweaters were also an expression of their love for natural fibres and their fascination with handwork.

I thought about my teaching style. I talk about the principles of knitting rather than offering step-by-step instructions or details about how to hold your yarn. I'm interested in the final outcome—no strands, not even over two stitches—and the process—no twists in the yarn, not even one. Otherwise, there wasn't much more to my workshops than all of us being together and sharing our stories. Some might call my style laid-back, West Coast, perhaps even British Columbian.

Reverse

MY STORY IS THE OPPOSITE of the boyfriend sweater story I've heard before, the one where the girl starts knitting her boyfriend a sweater and then by the time she finishes it they have broken up. Or where they break up halfway through the sweater and it gets left in a bag stuffed in a closet and is never finished.

The sweater I knit for my husband was the perfect symbol of our dreams of an exciting life together—fishing, hiking, exploring the outdoors. Once the kids came along, I rarely had time to knit. But bit by bit I kept working on it. I had to. It was the metaphor of our marriage. At some point later on, things got really bad between us. I couldn't face the sweater, so I put it away.

When my husband moved out, I packed his things in boxes and put them outside the front door for him to pick up. When I came across the sweater, I didn't know what to do with it. Was it his? Was it mine?

I realized the sweater had been such an important symbol of our relationship that I couldn't leave it unfinished. I wanted all the loose ends tied up. I wanted our separation to be a clean break. The only thing I could do with the sweater was finish it and give it to him. At first I was frustrated and angry. I couldn't get it done fast enough. But each time I sat down to knit, I would ponder our relationship. The stitches were like tiny episodes of our life together. The good and the bad, the dreams and the disappointments.

By the time I had sewed the pieces together and blocked the sweater, I decided I had made a mistake. When I gave it to my husband, I asked him to come home. And we have lived happily ever after.

Maybe not completely happily, and maybe we're not happy about every single thing, but that was more than twenty years ago. So we are doing pretty good.

ALBERTA

THE OTHER SIDE OF THE MOUNTAIN

TEX AND I SANG THE words we remembered to Gordon Lightfoot's song "Alberta Bound" as we headed east over the Crowsnest Pass. The tree cover thinned, the mountains dwarfed and gentle grassy foothills eased our way toward the Prairies. With no warning, a sign saying Welcome to Alberta appeared. We pulled over. I could see no obvious reason why British Columbia ended and Alberta began at that exact place on the road.

Borders have long been a challenge for me. Who said? Why? These arbitrary demarcations often defy the contours of lakes and streams, hills and icefields. Even when borders trace the actual terrain, they often divide watersheds and farms, and sometimes split people's backyards in two.

From the stories I've heard, Indigenous people distinguished land ownership or usage rights by making trails, drawing pictures and telling stories about fishing grounds, forests and foliage—a perfectly sensible system.

When Europeans arrived, they needed a way to override Indigenous land tenure and grant the land to immigrants for farming and development. At first they used water routes to mark territory, but agriculture lent itself to marking land in a different way. So when the new Dominion of Canada wanted sovereignty over settlement in the West, it imposed the Dominion Land Survey, the largest grid system in the world. I'm not advocating a return to the past, and perhaps Indigenous land tenure is not necessarily the best system in many modern circumstances. It's just that big squares on paper seem out of place and heavy-handed when applied to undulating and varied terrain.

The northern half of the border between Alberta and British Columbia neatly divides flat land. But when the colonial surveyors reached the Rocky Mountains they met their match, and the border takes a wiggly path as it heads south. Even the most orderly system has to give way to the region's extraordinary geography.

I stood in front of the Alberta sign and smiled for a photo. It was a pose I would repeat eight more times over the next month and a half. Tex reminded me that we had reached, or were near, the Continental Divide, the most important natural boundary on the continent. Between British Columbia and Alberta, the Divide runs along the high peaks of the Rockies, separating the watersheds that drain into the Pacific Ocean from those that drain into the Atlantic and Arctic Oceans. I leaned against the sign for a few more minutes, in awe at the significance of the place.

As we left coal-mining towns behind and descended the foothills, we talked about Alberta's importance in fuelling the country, from the hills of slag to the nodding donkey heads of the pumpjacks sucking oil. It wasn't long before we were in farming country, with grain crops and ranches that to my unaccustomed eyes appeared to be set on "repeat"— one looking more or less like the next.

Once we had passed through Pincher Creek, I realized that not only did Alberta lead the way in energy extraction and farming, but the province was also fusing its two economic strengths. Suddenly we were in the imposing presence of massive, giraffe-like windmills that swept across the landscape, like giant highways in the sky. Positioned to catch rivers of air, wind farms require us to add air to land and water when we are thinking about resources and territory.

Later in our road trip, driving through farm country in Ontario, it was similarly jarring to see hundreds of acres of glass and metal solar panels covering fields that once grew soybeans and alfalfa. Only time will tell what these windmills and panels will mean to wildlife, birdlife and even human life. For now I could only marvel at this vast presence in the landscape and wonder.

"I can't believe I'm saying this," I told Tex. "But, my goodness, how things have changed since I was a girl!"

ATHABASCA

NAMES, LIKE BORDERS, CAN TELL us a lot about ourselves—our ethnicity, the era in which we were born, our country of origin. They also make us who we are. My own name is a prime example. My mother wanted to give me a classic name like Mary or Catherine. My grandmother, an immigrant from England, stepped in and decided I should be called Sylvia Valerie, after two beautiful young women who were visiting at the time from the old country. But I am the youngest of five, and "Sylvia" was too much of a mouthful for my two-year-old sister, so like a lot of babies I got called Bub. The nickname stuck. At school, some of the teachers called me Sylvia, but to all the kids and to everyone else who knew me, I was Bub.

At seventeen I signed "Sylvia" on my marriage licence, but it was Bub who was getting married. Through a strange twist of fate, my first husband signed the licence as Carl, but it was also Bub I was marrying. As the sixth child in his family of twelve, his nickname was the same as mine. So we became Bub and Bub, Mr. and Mrs. Bub, Uncle and Auntie Bub, he-Bub and she-Bub.

I didn't become Sylvia until I was thirty-six. I had returned to school, and on my first day on campus a striking, sophisticated-looking woman a little older than I was extended her hand and said, "Hello, I'm Trish. I guess with all these kids around we need to stick together."

I couldn't say, "Hello, I'm Bub." The name didn't fit. For a split second I was stumped, and then I remembered:

"Hi, I'm Sylvia." I've been Sylvia ever since. Two of my older siblings continue to call me Bub. And sometimes I hear the name from old friends. I'm still Auntie Bub to hundreds of nieces and nephews, but Bub wasn't university material.

Did Sylvia make me a university student? Or did university make me Sylvia? Of course it had to happen. By the time I received a PhD in 2016, Dr. Bub just wouldn't have worked.

Perhaps the same applies to the name British Columbia —a constant reminder of the province's colonial past. Queen Victoria chose the name for what would become Canada's westernmost province to mark her claim on the Columbia District of the Hudson's Bay Company, disregarding the existing claims of the Indigenous residents of the territory. Now the province is attempting to reconcile with First Nations over the damage caused by colonization. In November 2019, British Columbia passed legislation to implement the United Nations Declaration on the Rights of Indigenous Peoples. Perhaps this signals that it's also time to change the name. I like the sound of Illahee, meaning "land," Tillikum, meaning "people," or Chako Kloshe, meaning "to become good." These words are from Chinook Jargon, the old trade language used in BC in the nineteenth century that enabled Indigenous, British and French people to understand each other. Perhaps this is an appropriate language from which to choose a new name for our province.

Princess Louise Caroline Alberta was the fourth daughter of Queen Victoria and her husband, Albert, Prince Consort. Princess Louise's husband, John George Edward Henry Douglas Sutherland Campbell, ninth Duke of Argyll and Marquess of Lorne, served as the fourth Governor General of Canada from 1878 to 1883. When Canada laid claim to the vast stretch of land between Manitoba and British Columbia and divided it into administrative districts in the 1880s, it needed to come up with names that severed the land's association with its original owners.

The governor general wanted to name one of the districts after his wife. Perhaps "Louisiana," or even "Carolina" of the North? In the end he decided on the name "Alberta," the name he often called her when he didn't shorten it to "Alba."

Alberta's a good enough European name. It comes from a German word meaning "noble and bright." When the province was formed in 1905 it was an amalgamation of two administrative districts, Alberta in the south and Athabasca in the north. If it had been my job to choose the name, I would have chosen Athabasca, an anglicized Cree word that has to do with grassy places and the reeds found on lake-shores. I'd have chosen it not only because of its musicality, but also because, like all Indigenous place names, it provides a meaningful connection to the land and conveys a love for place not found in names borrowed from foreign monarchs or travellers. It makes me wonder: if our names shape who we are, would Alberta be the province we know today if it had been called Athabasca? Would British Columbia be a different sort of place if it were called Illahee?

A Job

MY FAMILY EMIGRATED FROM NORTHERN India in 1975 when I was twelve. We moved to Nanaimo. I don't remember anyone knitting back home, but when we got to BC, all my aunties knit. Pretty soon my mom learned as well. At first she used a pattern, but later she memorized the stitches and she only needed a pattern when she made a new design.

My mother and my aunties knit sweater pieces—sides, backs, collars, sleeves. They piled them up in stacks on the table. My grandmother sewed the pieces together. Every week or so a buyer came around and brought boxes of wool. He took the sweaters and paid the women for their knitting. I don't know what they got paid. I don't think it was very much. But it was the only work my mom ever had in this country.

I never wanted to learn to knit. I wanted what I thought would be a real job. I don't think my mom wanted me to learn to knit either. Now that she's gone and I've moved to Calgary, I've been learning to knit. But I'm still keeping my real job.

FAUX PAS

TEX AND I CROSSED INTO Alberta on May 10, Mother's Day, something that would have passed us by if it hadn't been for the rose I was given at the bar where we stopped for supper.

"Do you miss your kids?" Tex asked.

I had to think about it.

"No. I miss the dinner the boys will be making for all the mothers in the family, but my kids are too old to miss."

Two of my children were almost forty—they would be more or less the same when I got home. But I did miss my seven grandchildren, especially the littlest ones. Six and a half weeks was one-third the length of Jack's entire life. He would have more hair and maybe even another tooth by the time I returned. Ella, who was three, would have learned several new dances and likely grown out of her pink cowboy boots.

I HAD COMMITTED MY FIRST road-trip faux pas just after supper as we drove along Highway 3 toward Pincher Creek. Tex is a great driver. Unless I'm afraid for my life, I don't grab the dash or gasp when a car comes too close. And honestly, I don't complain. The thing about this particular situation was that I wasn't complaining. I was simply stating the obvious.

"You are driving super close to that truck."

His face instantly turned to stone. Only the tips of his lips moved.

"Do you want to drive?" he said in a voice that came from the deepest pit of his stomach.

I said, "Sure," even though we had already established that he would do the driving. Tex doesn't only love to drive. He's driven solo across the country more times that he can count, and he doesn't like being a passenger. I love being a passenger. If I drove, how would I knit? We were a road-trip duo made in heaven. I had said "sure" just to avoid a confrontation. It worked. There was no argument. Instead, silence permeated the van until we stopped for gas.

He took the keys out of the ignition and put them in his pocket, forcing me to be the one to break the silence.

"I'll take the keys," I said, faking nonchalance.

He looked straight ahead.

"I thought you were asking me to drive."

"I asked if you *wanted* to drive. I didn't ask you to drive."

"Oh."

He was right, though it had meant the same thing to me.

"So, do you *want* me to drive?"

"No."

"Then I guess I don't need the keys?"

Done. Conflict over.

SHEEP

ONTARIO AND QUEBEC ARE CANADA'S number one and number two sheep-producing provinces. Alberta is a distant third. Nonetheless, I kept my eyes peeled, hoping to see a few flocks roaming the rangeland. But cowboys, not shepherds, dominate Alberta culture. Alberta is cattle country. Albertans' riding style, dress and cattle roping have captured the Canadian imagination from west to east. Shepherding has languished, as has the wool industry.

In Lethbridge we visited the western hub of the Canadian Co-operative Wool Growers. Tons of Canadian raw wool arrive here from the western provinces to be bundled and shipped. Seventy per cent is exported to China, with most of the remaining wool going to the United States, India, Japan, Britain and Western Europe. Because we have shut down the secondary industrial infrastructure needed to process it, only 10 per cent of Canada's wool goes to domestic mills. Our country's lack of attention to the wool industry seems ludicrous, though not surprising. In spite of how little sense it makes to me, it's like Alaskan salmon that gets processed in China and sold in grocery stores in the United States or shipping giant logs from the West Coast rainforests overseas to be milled and manufactured into flooring, guitars and pianos, which are shipped back to Canadians for sale.

"Surely there is a business case for rebuilding Canada's wool-processing industry," Tex posited as we drove. His ideas were reinforced when we met up near Edmonton with friends who owned a golf course.

Although he was amused that we were devoting a whole road trip to knitting, our friend told us he thought we were on to something big because he had heard that in the United States about 20 million women golf and more than 80 million knit.

I could find no verification for his assertion, and I don't know if the same proportions would apply in Canada. But even if it were half true, you would think someone would put a bit more effort into the wool industry.

KNIT-TING

SHARON MET US IN LETHBRIDGE at Knitting Time, located in a nondescript strip mall alongside the usual drugstore, western wear shop, liquor store and bank. On that Monday morning the shops looked all but deserted.

Sharon had contacted me several months earlier to see if I was interested in a machine knitting demonstration. Machine knitting is like the frozen bread dough of the knitting world. It smells something like homemade when it is baking, but when you're asked if you made the bread yourself, you are loath to admit that the dough was frozen, not made from scratch. Even though my daughter Joni pushes her home knitting machine beyond its limits to create art, I view the usual close-to-manufactured-looking knitting machine products as not quite knitting—one step away from the real thing.

However, and in spite of my aversion to any machine that is more complicated than a toaster, I thought if I watched closely, maybe Sharon could teach me something that would be helpful to Joni. I was eager to see the demonstration.

Sharon sat in front of the machine like a concert pianist. She adjusted the levers, then dragged her hand along the needles. I half expected to hear the trill of notes. Her explanations of how to pull the wool up, wrap it around, skip needles and pull the wool down became a background hum as I fixated on her hands. Just like several sets of double-pointed needles in the hands of an old Coast Salish woman, the knitting machine was an extension of Sharon's fingers. She turned sliding the shuttle into an art form as she made cables, hems and picoted edges. Unfortunately, I didn't listen closely enough to be able to pass along any of her tips. Joni would have to continue to rely on her trial-and-error method. But I came away from Sharon's demonstration with a whole new appreciation for knitting machines and the skill it takes to operate them.

Knitting Time sold a wide selection of acrylic, pastel-coloured, fingering-weight yarns to make baby sweaters and blankets. It had very few of the natural hand-dyed boutique yarns that were so prevalent in BC shops. I wondered if we had found the conservative knitters that I imagined would fulfill the stereotypes of the province of Alberta. But it soon became clear that the type of yarn people knit with did not affect their knitting enthusiasm.

For the workshop later that day, Sharon had set up the vacant shop next to hers with chairs and tables, and decorated the display window with skeins of bulky yarn, knitting baskets and double-pointed needles. The centrepiece was a stitch-by-stitch replica of the child's sweater shown in my book *Yetsa's Sweater*.

After we had lunch, I met with a reporter from the *Lethbridge Herald*. We sat across from each other at one of the tables, alone in the large room. He generously welcomed me to his city and then said, "I hear you are in town to do some kni*t-t*ing with the ladies."

His emphasis on the double *t* gave the word an unmistakably condescending tone. His comment brought to mind lonely grandmothers with little left to do but knit one, purl one, using yarn that no one would want to wear.

But when he continued, "I understand ladies still enjoy sitting around kni*t-t*ing and gossiping," I knew I had my work cut out for me. I didn't think a twenty-minute interview would be long enough for me to explain the new world of knitting in a way that would make sense to him. So I told him something about the important role knitting had played in the past, then explained I believed there was a current resurgence in the craft. I said something about my master's thesis on the history of Coast Salish knitters, which didn't seem to interest him, so I left it at that. Though I worried about what he would write, in the end he left out the gossiping part and refrained from patronizing the local knitters and me.

Sharon filled the room with people in the afternoon and again in the evening. There was no question Lethbridge knitters had a somewhat more old-fashioned approach than I had seen in BC, leaning away from modern yarns and designs. These were practical people, concerned less about style and more about wearability. But their stories matched anything I had heard to date.

There was no gossip in the room that day. Alberta had just experienced the political equivalent of an earthquake, and the knitters were shocked and outraged. The province's twenty-ninth election had taken place three days earlier, and it was only the fourth time Alberta had changed governments since it became a province in 1905. The NDP, winning for the first time, had unseated the Progressive Conservative party, which had won every election for the previous forty-four years.

"Who voted for them?" I asked the group.

"No one around here" was the prevalent sentiment.

If any of the knitters were happy about the political turn of events, they didn't let on.

"It's those people in Edmonton."

Later we found out that the Lethbridge knitters represented a strong dissenting voice, but it wasn't only Edmontonians who voted for change. The NDP won throughout the province, including both seats in Lethbridge. I realized the country song didn't have Alberta exactly right. The province was not a stereotypical monoculture, not even in terms of its politics.

The Yellow Sweater

THE WOMAN HAD IMMIGRATED TO Canada from Italy years ago. Still, Italy was home, and regular trips back kept her in touch with her family and friends. When she received word that her mother might have only a short time to live, she made arrangements to stay in Italy for several months, hoping she would be with her mother when she passed on. By the time she arrived, her mother was bedridden, and her mind had failed to the point that she didn't know her daughter's name.

MY MOTHER HAD BEEN AN expert knitter. She never sat down without having her knitting on her lap. She made my sister and me sweaters all through our lives. When my kids came along, she knit for them too. They loved getting packages of knitting in the mail.

In spite of Mom's poor health, it didn't seem right to see her hands still and folded on her lap. I thought she would prefer to knit, so I bought her some bright yellow yarn and cast on the stitches for a simple sweater. As I watched her awkwardly winding the wool around the needles I realized she had forgotten how to make even plain knit and purl stitches. She seemed to enjoy the activity, but her work was full of holes and knots and random loops of yarn.

I tried to show her how to hold her needles and how to put the yarn over and under in the same way she had showed me when I was a little girl. But all I did was frustrate her. By the end of each day the sweater had progressed into a bigger muddle of twists and bumps. Sometimes when she looked at her knitting,

Mom got a confused and worried look on her face. I could see sadness in her eyes.

So one night after putting Mom to bed, I unravelled the jumble and worked up several inches in smooth stockinette. In the morning she smiled when she picked up her knitting and said, "Oh, this is a beautiful yellow colour, don't you think? There are some things you just don't forget. I've never lost my touch."

Then she went on merrily twisting and knotting the yarn. From then on, each night after I had put her to bed, I untangled her work and pulled it back out. I put the stitches back on the needles and knit a few more inches onto the sweater. Each morning when she picked it up, she was so happy with her progress.

Mom held on longer than anyone expected, and I had to return to Canada. I put the yellow sweater, close to completion, away in the knitting basket. She died a few weeks later. I wasn't able to return for her funeral, so my sister finished the sweater. Now, whenever I go home to Italy, I wear the yellow sweater as a way to remember my mother's determination.

ARTIFACT

I MET THE KNITTERS FROM the Gilli-hook Heritage Knitters Guild in a small room in a seniors' recreation centre in Calgary. They explained that a gilli-hook is a traditional Nordic knitting device used to attach a ball of yarn to your shoulder so you can knit while doing other things.

I told the group about the note I had posted on Facebook saying I wanted to find the oldest sweater in the country and to hear the old sweaters' stories. I already had an appointment in Ontario to meet the oldest sweater I had heard about so far—a Cowichan sweater from the late 1930s that had been owned by a Japanese Canadian man who was displaced to an internment camp during World War II.

One of the knitters got up and said, "Please excuse me. I have to phone home."

When she came back into the room, she told us that her husband was on his way, bringing a sweater whose age rivalled the one in Ontario.

The knitter explained that her father was also a Japanese Canadian man who had been interned. His sweater had been bought in anticipation of his removal to northern Ontario to work in a road camp as part of the internment.

Japanese immigrants had never had an easy time in British Columbia. Even second-generation Japanese Canadians were viewed with suspicion that they were not truly committed Canadians. Following the attack on Pearl Harbor on

December 7, 1941, Japanese Canadians were categorized as "enemy aliens." The next day, fishing vessels they owned were impounded as a "defence measure." The rationale was that the fishermen could be working for the Japanese navy and spying on Canada's military. On February 24, 1942, the federal government passed an order-in-council that gave it the power to intern all "persons of Japanese racial origin." Japanese Canadian goods were impounded. People's property was sold, and families were relocated to camps across the country. By the end of the war the federal government had interned more than twenty-one thousand Japanese Canadians, most of whom had been born in Canada. Although the war ended in 1945, internees were not free to return to BC until 1949.

The woman's husband arrived, and she showed us her father's sweater. The sweater had bands of simple geometric designs unevenly placed on the body. It had been knit in the round and cut up the centre front, with the edges rolled under to make a finished edge along the zipper. The sweater appeared as old as any I had ever seen. It was worn thin but, surprisingly, had no frayed cuffs or edges. The once-grey wool had faded to a motley pale brown. Across the back, from shoulder to shoulder and below the neck, someone had darned cotton thread through the back of every stitch. On the inside the mend looked like a chain-link fence. On the outside it was almost invisible.

The woman believed her father's sweater had been bought second-hand, already worn thin across the shoulders. Her thrifty grandmother had likely reinforced the stitches so her son could get a few more years of warmth out of the garment.

Later, the woman sent me a note saying she had talked to her aunts but couldn't find out anything more about the sweater:

> So I guess that's where the story ends. I'm grateful for the small bit of the story that I do have. I'm not sure how other families were, but ours tended not to talk much about the things that happened during the war. It wasn't so much that the topic was actively avoided, but more a sense that the past was the past and we had moved on to better times. Seems a lot of heritage has slipped away as we have become more Canadian.

MECCA

ABOUT 100 KILOMETRES NORTHEAST OF CALGARY, on the rolling prairie between Carstairs and Linden, lies Custom Woolen Mills, the woolworkers' mecca of western Canada. It's one of the last traditional woolen mills in the country, with machinery dating back to the Industrial Revolution. The mill is housed in a collection of barns that surrounds a relocated train station. The owners, Fen Roessingh and Bill Purves-Smith, bought the station for one dollar and converted it into their family home.

You can send your raw fleece to Custom Woolen Mills and they will wash and card it and make it into yarn. They also produce their own lines of yarn, from single-strand to bulky six-strand. Their first choice, because of its unique qualities, is to use fleece from sheep raised in western Canada, but they also fill in their production runs with fleece from Ontario and Quebec. Although my family's company, Salish Fusion, uses Custom Woolen Mills yarn almost exclusively, I had never visited the operation or seen the owners face to face. Over the phone we had been working on developing a new six-strand twisted yarn that would reproduce the local handspun of earlier days in Coast Salish knitting. Now the first run was waiting for me at the mill, and I was excited about getting my hands on it. I needed to touch it.

The rhythmic clank and crank of old cast-iron machines, the pungent aroma of damp fleece and the whirr of the wooden spools met us at the door. I closed my eyes and imagined that if I had been alive a hundred years earlier, I would have searched out this place and breathed in the wonder. Maddy Purves-Smith, one of the second-generation owners of the mill, gave us a warm welcome. She reminded me of Joni, a perfect fusion of the old and the new. Maddy brings her university education, her modern ecological sensibility and her eclectic aesthetic to the ancient operation.

Generously, she took time to give us a guided tour, showing us the washing vats, carding machines, spinners, winders, a sock machine and a one-of-a-kind, handmade, flat-bed quilting machine. Maddy showed us how our new yarn had been made, and finally she took us upstairs to the yarn room.

There it was: a whole shelf bearing our new creation, cones of Prairie Sea Fusion, named to honour the yarn's West Coast and Prairie roots. Maddy gave us one pound of each natural shade. I felt as if I were meeting a new baby for the first time. I stroked the yarn and smelled it. I didn't count its toes, but I untwisted it to examine the strands, tugged on it to check its strength and picked out a few twigs.

After talking business with Maddy over tea and ginger cake, I said to Tex, "Let's get going. I have my needles in the van, and I need to knit something from this."

I picked up my maple-leaf dress and tossed it into the back seat. I pulled out a 7 mm circular needle from the pack, put the new yarn on my lap and I was ready to go.

ALBERTA KNITS

THERE IS NO WAY TO get lost in Alberta. The sun is usually shining, so you can find east and west by looking up into the endless blue sky, and it's not hard to spot signs pointing to Highway 2, which will take you north or south right up the middle of the province. Twenty minutes from the woolen mill we turned right on the highway and headed to our next three destinations.

Nowhere in the country had more knitters signed up for my workshops than the region within an hour's circumference of Edmonton. One group met in the library in Camrose. In Edmonton, we met in a community hall and in River City Yarns's upstairs classroom.

The most auspicious workshop location was the heritage building that housed the Wetaskiwin and District Heritage Museum. We sat in a horseshoe, filling the impressive main gallery beneath the two-storey ceilings of the early-twentieth-century building. The room was alive with mannequins dressed in velvet and lace, tartan and brogues. A wide staircase led up to second and third floors that displayed more costumes and historical artifacts.

Halfway through the Wetaskiwin workshop I received a call from Donna McElligott, the host of the CBC Alberta noon show. "I'm so sorry," Donna said. "I know I'm interrupting you, but I didn't want to let anyone else do this interview. I'm a big fan, and, oh my god, we are talking about knitting. How much better does it get?"

I thought to myself, I've a feeling we're not in Lethbridge anymore.

Once we were on the air, Donna opened by saying, "Most of the time we think about knitters as grandmotherly old women. But you are a blonde bombshell."

To go from being one of the "ladies who gossip" to "blonde bombshell" in the same province gave me a jolt. Neither label felt right for me, but I liked how "bombshell" sounded.

I can't give you solid statistics on the number of knitters in Canada or where they tend to congregate. But from the passionate response to our workshops in the Edmonton region, and given the relatively low population of the area, I wondered if I'd hit Canada's Knitting Central.

A final note for Lethbridgians: as we left Edmonton, heading east to Saskatchewan, we realized we had found the people who voted for the NDP, and they were happy to claim responsibility for the dramatic change of leadership in the province.

LONG FLAT

IT IS VERY CANADIAN TO question whether, in fact, there is such a thing as a Canadian identity. If we are looking for a grand, national story that fits us all—something that every Canadian can hear and say, "Hey, yeah, that's us, eh?"—then perhaps Canada does not have such an identity.

But the very idea of grand stories and big, overarching ideas of identity has come into question in recent decades. In the 2020s, national identities are not so much about all-encompassing attributes as they are the messy, conflicting, challenging interactions between a country and the diverse groups and individuals who live there.

Countries are like our West Coast Douglas firs: they don't reach their prime until they are a few hundred years old. Even now, at 150, Canada is still a teenager. Collectively, we are clearing up our bad complexion, losing our baby fat and learning to accept the colours of our skin. Canadians are no longer trying to explain who we are through the greatness of our railroads, our natural resources or our political system. We are finally getting to know our real history and beginning to acknowledge the ruptures and weaknesses in our country's past. I'm optimistic that we are becoming mature enough to appreciate the richness of our shared experiences, even when that is hard. Canada is getting more interesting as we share the stories that make us Canadian. It's like what I read on a T-shirt one day: KEEP CALM AND LISTEN TO THE STORY.

TEX AND I PULLED OVER in Lloydminster to say goodbye to Alberta. I stood in front of the welcome sign that read Canada's Border Town. When we first arrived in Alberta, I thought it resembled a foreign country. Its Texas-like swagger seemed better suited to its southern neighbour.

Stereotypes are not usually entirely wrong. There is often a kernel of truth in them, a hook that got the story started. There is no question that Alberta cowboys and oil donkeys appear to be Texan doppelgangers. But you can't blithely believe what you see. The province we left felt more like British Columbia's half-sibling. Could it be that our familial traits—exemplified in the environmental focus of Custom Woolen Mills, the rivers of wind farms, the lively political divide, our love of making things, our creativity and shared history—made us more alike than different?

Knots

WE WERE SOME OF THE lucky ones who escaped from Estonia after World War II when the Soviets took over. We lived in a displaced persons' camp in Germany. All we wanted to do was go home, but looking back, I don't think it was so bad. Even though there wasn't much to go around, we made do with what we had.

My mother took old sweaters that were frayed and full of holes beyond repair. She picked them apart and saved each piece of yarn, no matter how short it was. She tied the ends together with tight little knots. I remember holding my hands up while she wrapped the new lengths of yarn into skeins and put ties around them. She stuffed several of them at a time into a big pot on the stove for dyeing. I was so little I needed a chair pushed up close so I could stir the giant vat to make sure all the yarn was an even colour. Can you imagine a little girl so close to the flames? I held my arms up again when the dyed yarn was dry while my mother wound it into great big balls. I had never seen yarn that did not have joins. Inside my sweaters were maps of little matted, knotted tufts.

I came across a school photo of my class some years after those days in the camp. I was about twelve years old. I had such a smile of pride on my face. It still showed through more than sixty years later. When I looked closely at the photo, I remembered the blue sweater I was wearing. It was the first sweater I can remember that was made out of new wool. There were no knots on the inside. I was so proud of that sweater.

SASKATCHEWAN

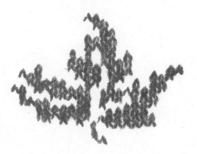

LOVE STORY

FROM THE BORDER IT WAS almost 300 kilometres to Saskatoon, our next destination. There wasn't much going on in that part of the country, just a few small towns I had never heard of: Marshall, Lashburn, Maidstone. The big sky we had marvelled at in Alberta seemed bigger still as it framed the ubiquitous Saskatchewan grain elevators and lonely farmhouses. Looking up, I got the feeling I had been dropped overboard and was swimming in the middle of the ocean. On the West Coast, hills and forests and omnipresent wisps of clouds comfortingly mask the immensity of the sky and the stark reality that only the force of gravity pins humans to the planet and keeps the abyss at a distance. Then, at some point along the prairie highway, I spotted the first sign for North Battleford.

Growing up in the Snobelen family, we had an affinity for Ontario. It was easy to recognize an uncle or cousin who came west because we all had a similar fair-haired and blue-eyed Snobelen look. Something about the demeanour and attitude of our visitors connected me to their stories of southern Ontario, the chosen lands of our original settler ancestors from Alsace-Lorraine.

But Ontario and Germany are the story of only one half of the Snobelen side of my family. The union that produced my father, Don Snobelen, took place in North Battleford. It was in that out-of-the-way place that Joseph Snobelen and Eva Macpherson found each other, married and had their first son. While I could not feel any twinge of prairie in my blood as the road signs registered the diminishing distance to my father's birthplace, I tried to imagine what it must have been like for my grandparents in 1917, the year he was born.

When I was young, I heard bits and pieces of stories about a sod house, banks of snow that covered the windows, the stubborn prairie soil and the Canadian government's promise of prosperity in the vast "free for the taking" West that lured Joseph Snobelen from Ontario but never panned out. However, the story I share here was told to me by Old Joe Snobelen, as my grandpa was often called, just months before he died of congestive heart failure. I can't attest to the veracity of the details, but from the determination on Grandpa's face that day, I can assure you that this was a story Old Joe had to tell.

He sat in his recliner at my parents' house, where he lived out his last days, and caressed the crook of his cane. As the words left his lips, he appeared to marvel at how his life might have been different if the events he was recounting had never taken place.

He told me that he had not been Eva Macpherson's first choice for a husband. My grandma was only seventeen years old when she left Napton on the Hill in England's Midlands and booked passage across the Atlantic to New York. As a kid, I had seen a photo of Eva, a stunning blonde, blue-eyed wisp of a girl, sitting on bales of hay above two less beautiful girls and wrapped in a sash that said "Napton on the Hill Queen of the May." Her willowy arm was held high, her hand cupped in a wave as if she were the Queen of England riding in the back of a Rolls-Royce.

Eva left her family's bakery business and set off for America because she had received a proposal of marriage from a man named Clayton. According to Grandpa, Clayton was a rich American who had visited Napton and wooed Eva, impressing her enough to risk the trans-Atlantic journey with the expectation of meeting her betrothed on the docks of New York, marrying him and living a posh and privileged life—a life she thought would befit the Queen of the May.

On the January day her boat arrived, a winter storm was raging on the East Coast. Exactly what happened on that dock isn't clear. Grandpa provided no details, other than to say that Clayton wasn't there. Eva had left her family and braved the ocean voyage, only to be stood up. As all of us who knew Eva in her later life could imagine, she did not take well to the indignity of the situation.

Grandpa said Eva didn't wait long before she headed to the train station and bought a ticket to the only other place on the continent where she knew someone. The McAdams family, who had also visited Eva's family in Napton, lived in North Battleford, Saskatchewan. When she arrived after what must have been a gruelling journey, and still stung by the rejection, Eva met a young stranger, Joe Snobelen, the owner of a successful livery business. Sometime later the two married.

Grandpa's voice lowered and his words slowed as he told me he sold the livery business and moved thirty-five miles north to Mullingar with his new bride to fulfill his dream of homesteading. That's where my father was born in a howling January blizzard, two months premature and struggling for his life.

"He couldn't have weighed more than a couple of pounds," Grandpa said, shaking his head.

My grandparents lined a box with straw and put baby Don in the warming oven to keep him alive. Grandpa said there were no other women around to help. My grandmother was unable to breast-feed her baby, so the two of them dripped cow's milk from a spoon into the mouth of their tiny son.

The family braved unrelenting hard work and poverty for three or four years before packing their bags and moving to the friendlier clime of Saltspring Island, BC, where Joe found a job in a lumber mill.

Grandpa told me the rest of the story, but he didn't have to. I remembered, as a little girl, seeing my grandmother dressed in her finest, sitting under the apple trees, having tea on occasion with a dapper gentleman named Clayton while Grandpa worked out back in the garden. Much later, when Grandpa and Nana had sold their house and come to live with my parents, a white-haired Clayton continued to arrive from time to time. Again Grandpa would go out into the garden so Nana could entertain her guest in privacy. Clayton paid his last visit to Eva as she lay in an extended care hospital, after she had broken her hip and lost her memory to dementia.

Old Joe Snobelen knew he was closing in on his own final days when he told me this story. Each breath gurgled with the stewy-lung sound of heart failure.

"He told Eva that after his wife died sometime in the 1950s, he promised himself that he would find Eva. When he found her, he promised to wait for her," Grandpa said. He heaved his lumbering frame forward and rested his head in his hands. Resignedly, he wagged his head from side to side. "He was waiting for me to go so he could marry her." But Old Joe had outlived Eva, thwarting Clayton's dream.

Since then I have wondered if the resentfulness I knew in my grandmother was because she never got over being stood up at that New York dock. Or was it the bitter Saskatchewan winters her family had spent in their sod shack, or birthing her first son in such unpleasant circumstances? Or was it because she had chosen Old Joe instead of George McAdams, her other suitor, who would have given her a more comfortable life than my grandfather did?

JUST OUTSIDE NORTH BATTLEFORD, WE pulled into a Tim Hortons. The building was plunked in the centre of what would once have been acres of alfalfa or canola and was now flagged for commercial development. I imagined the large plots would soon be home to Walmart or Costco, with their fields of parking lots. Tex pointed the van away from the building, and we sat for a few minutes to watch the deep orange sky soften to a golden peach glow. I could understand why prairie dwellers love their wide-open spaces.

I had wanted to have dinner downtown so I could walk along the main street of North Battleford and sit on the step of the old post office, which was built in 1911. I wanted time to imagine young Joe Snobelen posting letters to his family in Blenheim, telling them that farming in northern Saskatchewan was nothing like tilling the fertile fields of southwestern Ontario. I wanted time to empathize with beautiful Eva as she handed the postmaster her letter to her brothers and sisters in Napton: "Clayton didn't show up.

I'm in northern Saskatchewan, staying with the McAdams family. This is not at all what I had imagined." But we were road weary, and it was still more than an hour's drive to Saskatoon.

"Tim Hortons will have to do—again," I huffed.

I ordered what was becoming my go-to dinner on the road: a whole-wheat bun, a bowl of chili and a bag of hot potato chips to share. The food was somewhat satisfying (especially the potato chips), but it would soon start to stick to my hips and cheeks in a way I resented.

Once we were back on the road, I thought about how very Canadian my Snobelen family's story was: our resettlement from Europe to this new land we assumed was our own, moving from Ontario to the Prairies to the West Coast, until there was no farther to go. I thought about how I had contributed to the Canadianness of our family when I married Carl and had children who were a blend of the original Coast Salish residents of the land and the newcomers. Then I thought about how many Canadians, like my children, are a fusion of the gritty endurance, dreams and resolve of travellers from abroad and the patient, tough, grounded, persistent, earth-connected ways of Indigenous people.

We were only three provinces into this great land mass, and I already knew that if there was a Canadian identity, it wasn't something I could pull out like a passport. Our identity is in the anticipation of great things and the disappointments that often come instead. It's in the sinew that holds us together and the fissures that keep us apart. It's in the stories we tell about ourselves.

Prayers

I TOOK UP KNITTING PRAYER shawls when my mother went into a long-term care home. They are beautiful and useful, comforting for the old people and very therapeutic for me.

———

A WOMAN BROUGHT ALONG A tattered sweater she had knit for her father fifty years earlier. "Now he's been gone for almost ten years," she said, burying her face in the sweater and drawing in a long breath as if hoping to catch the lingering scent of her father. "It's my favourite reminder of him."

———

ONE WOMAN CAME INTO A workshop wearing a droopy, ragged sweater. "I know," she said. "It's like a big dog in a little apartment. It doesn't work. But it belonged to my best friend. It fit her much better than it fits me. When she passed away I rescued it and gave it a home."

———

A WOMAN WITH A HEAVY Scottish accent told us she had learned to knit when she was eight or nine years old. She has knit cables, colourwork, sweaters, shawls, socks: you name it, she's knit it. She's used yarn from featherweight to bulky. "I can't even count how many things I have knit, how many gifts I've given, how many people I've taught to knit, how many nights I've spent knitting when I couldn't sleep because I was worried about a sick kid or our bills and then my husband, right up until he passed away."

◯

WE HAD A MESSY DIVORCE. There were so many bad days. I thought it couldn't get worse than the day he took his clothes out of our room and left. But my heart broke when he returned a few days later with the sweater I had knit for him. He gave it to me and said he couldn't keep it. The emotions wrapped up in that sweater were too hard even for him to take.

◯

I CAME FROM PAKISTAN TWO years ago and could only speak a few words of English. I took language classes at night, but I was no good at it. No good at all. Then one day I went into this wool shop to find something to knit. The owner was so kind and patient. She invited me to a knitting group. It is quiet in the room where we meet. People talk to each other gently so I can listen. They know I want to learn English, so they ask me questions. I am learning how to make conversation while I knit.

TIME OFF

OUR FIRST CHOICE IN SASKATOON would have been to stay at the King Edward Hotel, which opened its doors in 1907. The King Edward had been the most elegant hotel on the prairies. It housed travellers from Europe who visited prairie towns in search of land and business opportunities during the Saskatchewan boom in the early twentieth century—perhaps even Eva Macpherson on her way to North Battleford. But the original hotel hadn't survived a fire in 1961, so we stayed in Saskatoon's *new* most elegant hotel— the Bessborough. The Canadian Pacific Railway didn't start building the Bessborough until 1929, seven or eight years after Grandpa and Nana left the prairies and boarded the train to British Columbia.

We splurged on a room with a view of the South Saskatchewan River. But unlike my grandmother, who would have appreciated the crystal chandeliers, fine china and silverware, I find grand hotels are usually too grand for me. Don't get me wrong. I love high ceilings, coved trims, luxurious cashmere carpets and squeaky old brass door hardware. But I can sleep just as well on a box spring and mattress in a room with a side table and a clothes stand. My only criteria are that the room doesn't smell like chemical cleaners or the previous occupants. The most important feature of the Bessborough was that our room had sash windows that opened.

The drive from North Battleford to Saskatoon had given me time to finish the child's sweater I had started at Custom Woolen Mills using the new Prairie Sea Fusion twisted six-strand. At three stitches to an inch, the sweater was quick to knit, and by the time I'd woven the ends in I was itching to wash it. I needed to know if the wool would live up to my high expectations. I had knit the little sweater with a 7 mm circular needle, the size I used when I made sweaters with my own handspun. For Coast Salish knitters, nine double-pointed 7 mm or 6.5 mm needles were pretty much universally the needles of choice. This was the first time I had knit bulky handspun-like wool on a circular needle, and I was worried about the strength of the joint that connected the cable to the needle ends.

Knitting with raw handspun, or in this case twisted six-strand, is hard work—on your fingers, your back and your tools. Casting onto nine double-pointed needles (also known as DPNs) and then moving from one needle to the next eight times on each round might sound like a nightmare to those unfamiliar with the method, but it has advantages when you are using heavy wool. Your work stays more buoyant; it doesn't hang from your needles like it does on a circular. Nor are you constantly pulling the stitches around to the ends of your needles. DPNs are longer than the ends of a circular too, so your work feels more stable. And on a circular, the cable doesn't feel strong enough to carry a heavy sweater of sticky lanolin-laden wool, making the stitches more resistant.

With a circular, however, you only have to find one needle; you don't lose your stitches at the end, as you do with DPNs; and there are no more transitions.

In spite of newfangled tools and materials like circular needles and machine-twisted wool, the little sweater I'd made looked exactly like the Cowichan sweaters I had purchased for my shop for decades. The little sweater felt stiff in the same way the sweaters I bought had felt when they came in without being washed. I was sure that Coast Salish knitters back home would love the new wool.

And once I had finished the sweater and weighed the advantages of the DPNs against those of the circular, the circular won. Since then, my DPNs have been relegated for use only on collars, bind-offs and smaller projects.

WHEN I USED TO BUY sweaters, I would block them myself before I zippered them. One at a time, I'd dump them into the kitchen sink, filling the sink with hot water and adding a dollop of Sunlight dish detergent. I would knead the fabric until I was sure the water had penetrated, let the sweater sit for ten minutes, then rinse it under warm running water. Next I would haul the sopping, heavy, dog hair–smelling lump out of the sink, put it into a large bowl and transfer it to my washing machine. I centred the weight first (otherwise my poor washer would sound like an old car with a flat tire) and then put the machine on spin for a few minutes. When that was done, I'd pull the pliable fabric back into shape. Finally, I'd inhale deeply—there's nothing like the scent of a barnyard.

So when Tex and I got into our room at the Bessborough, the first thing I did was plug the bathroom sink, put in the child's sweater, empty in the little container of hotel shampoo and fill the sink with hot water.

Once the sweater had soaked, though, I found out how much I needed my washing machine. Blocking instructions say to squeeze out as much water as you can, then roll your garment in a towel to extract the rest of the water. That's easier said than done when you are using twisted six-strand. Tex took one end of the towel and I took the other, and we wrung the little sweater until dirty brown water dripped into the bathtub.

"Enough now," I said.

Even though we had squeezed the sweater to our limit, it was still heavy and wet. Then I got an idea. It had been a sunny day, and although it was now dark, the air was warm. I hung the sweater out the window and pulled the sash down to pin it to the windowsill.

The next morning as we walked along the river trail, we looked up at the Bessborough, and there, like a secret beacon, hung my little sweater. Other strollers must have wondered what message the travellers on the fifth floor were sending.

SIWASH

I HAD A PARTICULAR MISSION for the Saskatchewan leg of our trip. Armed with some preliminary research, I was on the hunt for answers about "Siwash" sweaters. For years I had heard from First Nations people in Saskatchewan that their women knit sweaters they called "Siwash," which resembled Cowichan sweaters. I wanted to know what sort of sweaters they were, and if the women in Saskatchewan had learned to knit them from Coast Salish women. I wanted to know if there had been a knitting industry on the Prairies like there had been on the Coast.

On several earlier business trips to First Nations in Saskatchewan, I had asked around for anyone who could tell me about local knitters. I felt guilty using the word "Siwash." It's a term in Chinook Jargon meaning "an Indigenous man" (or sometimes a woman) and it is considered a derogatory word on the West Coast.

Chinook is a nineteenth-century pidgin made up of elements of several West Coast Indigenous languages, as well as English and French. It was used for trade in the Pacific Northwest from Oregon to British Columbia and could be heard as far north as Alaska. Although the language had a limited vocabulary, some Indigenous people who lived in settler communities spoke it almost exclusively. By the late nineteenth century it was estimated that more than 100,000 people could speak Chinook.

As the settler population increased, most words identifying Indigenous people came to embody racist ideas and so were struck from the lexicon of many British Columbians.

Names aside, I had sweaters I needed to investigate. Interestingly, the word "Siwash" did not appear to have derogatory connotations on the Prairies, and most Indigenous people brightened up when asked about the sweaters. Some told me about a mother, a grandmother or an auntie who knit.

One man laughed at my question and said, "We thought the sweaters Mom knit were made of wool from buffalos. We all called them 'Siwash,' but she called them 'White Buffalo' sweaters. The knitting patterns she used had a little icon of a buffalo on them. I remember that."

He recalled his mother knitting for everyone in the family but not selling her knitting, at least not to anyone outside of his community. "Sometimes she'd get paid for knitting one for our cousins, but not most of the time."

People said that the sweaters they remembered looked like "those sweaters from Vancouver Island," but that was about all I had been able to find out.

In preparation for the Great Canadian Knitting Tour, I apologized about the use of the term and then posted two questions on Facebook: "What's a Siwash sweater?" and "Why are they generally found only in Saskatchewan?"

Some people who responded to my post said they thought Siwash sweaters were just Cowichan sweaters known by a different name. A woman from Yorkton explained that Saskatchewanians had had a close relationship with Vancouver Island in the past because many farmers did not heat their farms in the winter. Once the prairie cold set in, they shuttered their barns and houses. Then, instead of going south to Mexico or Florida, prairie snowbirds flocked to the West Coast. Hotels and other businesses in Victoria thrived by providing rooms until the spring thaw set in and the farmers returned home to their fields.

Although prairie people were used to cold weather, they needed a way to keep warm on the damp coast. "Indian" sweaters were the answer—or "Siwash" sweaters, as they were called back home. The woman from Yorkton said that when the farmers returned and sang the sweaters' praises, their neighbours placed orders to be filled the following winter.

"That's what happened in my family," the woman wrote. "So when my generation went off to university in the 1970s, we were the lucky recipients of the 'must have' fashion from the West."

Saskatchewanians didn't only love wearing these sweaters; they also loved knitting them. Theirs weren't handspun, make-it-up-as-you-go sweaters like the Cowichans. Prairie knitters reproduced the sweaters using store-bought yarn and patterns from either Mary Maxim or White Buffalo, which actually called a few of its patterns "Siwash."

From my Facebook research, my theory when I arrived in Saskatchewan on our tour was that there wasn't a specific Indigenous connection to the Siwash sweaters. Indigenous knitters in Saskatchewan, like other knitters in the province, liked the bulky sweaters and knit them for their families. Knitters who were especially industrious sold their work, and in the 1970s and '80s there were plenty of customers. Siwash sweaters were either Cowichan or White Buffalo sweaters by another name.

I was eager to meet Saskatoon knitters and verify my research findings. I wanted to test my theory about words' meanings changing over borders and across cultures. I could feel that my search for the Siwash sweater's identity was nearing an end.

Tex had brought along Google directions to Prairie Lily Knitting, which seemed straightforward until we found ourselves way out of town in a light industrial neighbourhood. The last place we expected to find a yarn shop was in a commercial mall alongside furniture stores and warehouses. But by this time we were beginning to understand that yarn shops were not necessarily on main streets nor dependent on walk-ins. Yarn shops are destinations, and Prairie Lily had been operating successfully in what appeared to us to be an out-of-the-way district for more than seven years.

"Knitters find us," the owner said when we got there. "They don't let the location get in their way of getting yarn."

A few people brought their Siwash/White Buffalo /Icelandic sweaters to the workshop. Most of them had never given much thought to the histories of their sweaters. A few knitters confessed they found the colour combinations gaudy and the designs bordering on tacky.

As in all my workshops, I shared stories about Coast Salish knitters, showed my samples of old knitting and described the differences between the West Coast sweaters and those from White Buffalo and Mary Maxim patterns. I demonstrated my own fusion-style knitting and taught what I now call Intuitive Colourwork.

"Of course, this colourwork was not invented by Coast Salish knitters," I said. "Many knitters use it. But it is the colourwork used most often by Coast Salish knitters, and there doesn't seem to be any other knitting tradition that uses it so exclusively."

My cross-country knitting tour was already softening my concepts about origins and ownership. The identity of Cowichan sweaters has been fiercely contested on the West Coast, and I have written much about that. But the tradition incorporates other traditions from around the globe that radiate in the imaginations of knitters everywhere. I wondered: is identity something you make for yourself or something imposed on you by others that you start to believe in and then become?

By the time we got to Saskatoon, I was considering Cowichan sweaters as the material manifestation of inspiration, and as an inspiration in turn for new knitting styles, whatever name was assigned to them.

When all was said and done, the Saskatoon knitters agreed on one thing. Whether they liked the colour combinations and designs or not, and whatever name they knew them by, their sweaters were Canadian, and that was reason enough for the knitters to love them.

Cool

WHEN I WAS IN HIGH school and university in the 1970s, Cowichan sweaters were the absolutely cool thing to own, and not just for young people. A couple of shops in Saskatoon sold them. When I was in first year at the University of Saskatchewan, my mom phoned and said, "Buy your dad a Cowichan sweater for Christmas and I'll reimburse you." They were expensive. I paid something like fifty dollars or seventy dollars for Dad's sweater. This is when a month of board and room cost seventy dollars.

Saskatoon was a great place for Cowichan sweaters. Hippies and radicals were running the show here. I don't think the sweaters were such a big deal at the University of Regina.

My friend took a lot of her grade school in BC because her dad went out there every winter to work in a mill. The families came back to Saskatchewan for seeding and harvest. Some probably picked up their Cowichan sweaters while they were out there in BC. I don't know for sure.

MANITOBA

HALFWAY

FIND 64 DEGREES, 18 MINUTES, 41 SECONDS NORTH and 96 degrees, 4 minutes, 8 seconds west, and you will be close to the geographical centre of Canada. Baker Lake, Nunavut, is proud to call itself the core of the country. But when you are on a Canadian road trip, you know you are getting close to the centre when you see signs pointing to Winnipeg. Longitudinally, Taché, Manitoba, forty kilometres southeast of the capital, at 96 degrees, 40 minutes, 0 seconds west, is dead centre.

We arrived in Winnipeg on May 20, with exactly three weeks of our road trip behind us and three weeks ahead. Feeling tired, I asked Tex, "What is the point of this tour again? Why are we driving across the country?"

"Well." He always pauses after saying "well." It gives him another few seconds to gather his thoughts.

"Well." His second pause made me think he was probably tired too, and maybe not quite sure why he had agreed to spend six weeks on the road. "Something about finding out how Canada knits. And didn't you want to see what knitting says about being Canadian?"

"Hmmm."

What better place to think about being Canadian than in Winnipeg, site of the old Hudson's Bay Company fort, Fort Garry, and of Canada's only revolution. The rebels lost the 1869–70 confrontation that pitted Louis Riel, his Métis followers and their short-lived provisional government against the newly formed Government of Canada, so mainstream history has reduced the event to a rebellion. As happens with all failed revolts, the uprising was subdued, but the issues didn't go away. Riel petitioned the government again in 1884 over the lack of Métis representation in the government of the North-West Territories (present-day Alberta and Saskatchewan) and to demand full title to Métis lands. The lack of government interest and cooperation resulted in another armed Métis resistance. For his part in the rebellion, Louis Riel was tried for high treason, and after several postponements of his execution he was hanged at Regina on November 16, 1885.

Did I call Riel a rebel? He was executed like a rebel. But as with all names history attaches to people, they don't necessarily tell the real story. New Canadian histories have turned the tables on the old narrative. Once seen as a villain, the new Riel is a hero, and Canada is being put on trial in the hearts and minds of many Canadians for its villainous treatment of the Métis people.

I am certain of one thing—Canada should have taken Riel more seriously. The government would have done well to settle the issue in the nineteenth century, because the subjugation of the Métis and First Nations peoples has challenged the country's legitimacy ever since. Now, after 150 years of land grabs, broken treaties, alienation from natural resources, residential schools, unthinkable living conditions and poverty, Indigenous people in Canada are mounting another revolution. This time they are doing it in a truly Canadian manner—they are being smart and determined but polite. There are no strident leaders, no guns, no threats of violence. Instead, there is a generation of young, educated

Indigenous people who are learning their languages, revising their histories and reinvigorating their cultures. This generation intends to settle past issues and improve the lot of their people, improving all of Canada in the process.

Pulling into Winnipeg felt like wading into the deeper waters of Canada's political identity. Nowhere else in the country would we see so much evidence of the persistent fissures the old conflicts had created in Canadian society.

Tammy from the Manitoba Craft Council, who had organized the workshops, said she wanted us to get to know the city in two stops. The first event was held at a mall, in a room tucked in the back at McNally Robinson Booksellers. The store was filled with moms and their kids at storytime, older people reading newspapers and students leafing through books. The hushed busyness appeared to have been choreographed respectfully around the stacks of books, magazines and other upscale odds and ends. My sold-out class of middle-aged women sat around a long table in the dark, wood-panelled room—a classic scene from Canadian suburbia.

Later that day we walked up Main Street to the Arts Cooperative where my evening class was to take place. The sidewalk out front was scattered with people walking aimlessly. Others sat on the concrete, leaning their backs against the old buildings.

A man who looked about my age held out his hand half-heartedly. "Anything you got would help," he said. "Just looking to get myself something to eat."

This section of the city was obviously an Indigenous homeless neighbourhood. I had the sense the place was as much a living room as a public space. Things meant to be private were exposed to the glare of passers-by. Some non-Indigenous people appeared to share the neighbourhood, but most hurried through.

Eleven per cent of Winnipeg's population is Indigenous—the highest proportion of any major city in the country—but 71 per cent of the city's homeless identify as Indigenous. Many people living on the streets in Winnipeg have migrated from First Nations communities in the North. Perhaps they came to the big city for a visit or school or the promise of a job and never went home. Maybe there was no house for them at home either.

The Arts Cooperative was in an old building that might once have housed a print shop or furniture maker. The interior brick walls were clean, but they looked as if they hadn't been painted for decades. There was a small front window onto the street, but the back of the interior, where the workers would have been, retreated like a cave into darkness. In the early twentieth century, Winnipeg was the Chicago of the North, a hub of distribution where goods from the East were shipped to the outports in the West. Jewish, Ukrainian, Icelandic and other European immigrants brought their skills and trades and settled in the city, establishing businesses in buildings like the one we were using.

Some people might have called the area industrial chic, but it looked more "rugged abandoned" to me. The small businesses once run by craftspeople have vacated the neighbourhood, leaving only traces of their industry: iron hooks driven into the brick walls, gullies and troughs worn smooth in the concrete floors, pulleys attached to raw timbers. The neighbourhood felt uncomfortably resettled with a palpable sense of the subjugation of Indigenous peoples that has continued since Louis Riel.

The class that met on Main Street was smaller than the earlier gathering at the bookstore. The participants were mostly young and not-so-young artists and service workers who didn't mind spending the evening on the "other side of town."

Even a few days in Winnipeg made me want to return. I had a visceral sense of its multi-racial roots, the Cree, French, English and European threads that make up the fabric of Manitoba society. If I could understand Winnipeg, I thought, I'd get to the heart of some of my questions about Canadian identity.

War Stories

I LEARNED TO KNIT IN Germany during World War II. We spent many days down in the bunkers without much to do—without much of anything. We straightened out broken bicycle spokes and used them for knitting needles. We unravelled gunnysacks that had once been filled with rice and flour. Then we knit up hats and mittens. It felt good. I think knitting held the promise that even when everything was being destroyed, things could be put back together.

I LIVED IN HOLLAND DURING the German occupation in World War II. All the wool went to Germany, so we had no yarn. We used to go out into the fields and pull tufts of wool off the bushes. We collected it in sacks until we had enough to spin and knit something.

DURING THE WAR I WAS a young teenager. There was a program at our church to get us all to knit squares for blankets. They sent them overseas. We were given needles and yarn and told to knit thirty-five stitches and as many rows as needed to make it square. I remember sitting on the street curb and knitting with a German friend of mine. We would say one, two, three, start! We would race to see who could knit her square the fastest. She won every time. She knit continental, and I knit the British way. I don't think you can ever beat continental knitters for speed.

WHEN I WAS ELEVEN OR twelve I belonged to a girls' group in Montreal. It was during the Korean War. People donated miscellaneous yarn, and we were all given needles. We had competitions to see who could knit the most squares. The group leader sewed them all together and made blankets and then sent them to Korea.

"TAKE THIS SCARF IF YOU are cold . . . or if you like it. Chase the Chill." So reads the tag on the brightly coloured scarfs tied on trees in downtown Winnipeg.

I got the idea of knitting scarfs for people in need, regardless of income, from a woman in the States. She had started Chase the Chill as a way to combine good works with art and knit bombing. I knew it would be perfect for Winnipeg so I got a group together up here. The first year the group knit 56 scarfs, the next year 220. We tied them to trees on a Saturday, and by Sunday morning there were only thirty left. We took them down and donated them to a homeless shelter. We didn't want them to be wasted. The idea was to create something you think is beautiful and useful, and then share it with someone who also thinks it's beautiful and useful.

WHAT'S MY STORY?

JOURNALISTS WANT STORIES, AND WHEN Doug Spiers, a writer for the *Winnipeg Free Press*, heard that sweaters could be stories, he pulled the old Cowichan his parents had given him when he was a teenager out of a trunk and brought it along to the workshop at McNally Robinson.

Doug is something of a local celebrity, so the twenty knitters around the table were attentive when he patted his stomach, tossed his sweater on the table and said, "I'm too fat for it now. But here it is. Tell me the story."

It felt like the challenge my supervisors had thrown down when they brought their Cowichan and Cowichan-like sweaters to my master's thesis defence. I had written my thesis on the history of the Coast Salish knitters, and if I was going to claim to be a knitting historian, they thought I should be able to tell them something about their sweaters. Like the professors, Doug expected me to interpret his sweater's geometric designs as if they were talismans that held mystical meanings—a secret code with deep Indigenous significance. He thought I would be able to "read" the designs, leading him to where the sweater was knit or even to the knitter herself.

The centre design on his sweater was the ubiquitous Greek key, found on ancient Coast Salish baskets but also, as the name denotes, in various forms across the globe and through history since before the time of the Babylonians. I told Doug that the design on his sweater was universal. The most interesting thing it "said" was that knitters, weavers, mosaic artists, floor layers, painters, silversmiths, basket makers and many other craftspeople from around the world have loved the Greek key since the beginning of time as we know it.

Yet I was excited, because Doug's sweater did, in fact, tell a story, although not the sort of story he was expecting. His sweater was a poor specimen of Cowichan knitting. The stitches were loose and irregular, and the joins at the collar had gaping holes. The yarn that had once been grey and white had faded nicely to a dappled chocolatey brown and deep cream. But the design colour was as black as the day the sweater was knit. It jarred my senses, like a note played out of tune.

The discontinuity looked ghastly, and it brought me back to the days in the mid-1970s when I would visit Laura, my mother-in-law, and sit with her to knit.

"Your sweater's story is not in the design. It is in the black wool used in the design," I told Doug. He looked confused. "Good dark wool for the design work was always at a premium. But by the 1970s there was such a high demand for Coast Salish sweaters that there was a serious shortage of local dark wool. To solve the problem, sweater dealers imported dyed black roving from New Zealand. I remember going down to my mother-in-law's place and seeing her knitting the jet-black, wiry, imported wool into an otherwise natural-coloured sweater. Even then it looked out of place but she was excited about it. 'Look, they've got all the black wool we'll ever need downtown,' she told me.

"'But it's dyed,' I protested. 'Aren't Coast Salish sweaters supposed to be knit with undyed natural local handspun?'

"She was unfazed by what I thought was a cultural indiscretion."

Doug looked interested but confused.

I told him that I was like a lot of non-Indigenous people who had decided "authentic" Cowichan sweaters should use only undyed yarn. This prescription did not come from the knitters but from what Laura called "outsiders." In fact, sweaters that date back to close to the beginnings of the tradition sometimes had coloured yarn, or even cotton scraps, inserted at the knitter's whim.

Laura, like the early knitters, hated anyone telling her what to knit or how to knit it. She loved to work new ideas into her knitting, new shapes, new yarns, new designs. She only stuck to the prescribed Cowichan sweater format because those sweaters were what people expected, and they were easier to sell.

"So what does all this have to do with my sweater?" Doug asked.

"The dealers only imported this particular type of roving for a few years," I said. "It was too black, and the dye didn't match the subtle, natural colours the knitters were using. Sometimes the black dye bled into the other colours, and the black wool was also a different texture than the local wool. After a while, no one liked it."

"So are you telling me that your mother-in-law might have knit this sweater?"

"No, she was a much more skilful knitter. I'm saying that I can date this sweater almost to the year. It is an interesting part of the evolutionary story of the Cowichan sweater. The knitters were adaptive, but not everything they tried worked out well, and your sweater is an example of one of their not-so-successful adaptations."

"So my sweater might be ugly, but it's significant?"

I told Doug that old sweaters are like old people. They are not necessarily wonderful; they have simply survived. Doug's sweater reminded me of body parts that have been surgically altered. Even when everything around them begins to fade, altered parts stay as fresh as the day of surgery.

"Your sweater is an important historical document. If you ever want to get rid of it, let me know. It's a great illustration for the stories I tell."

A few days later, when I read Doug's article, I realized that journalists were reshaping my personal identity as we crossed the country. I had been an old lady gossiper in Lethbridge and a blonde bombshell in Wetaskiwin. In Winnipeg I became a knitting crusader, guru and legend. Later writers would add to the list of categories, describing me as a storyteller, a knitting historian, an expert, an evangelist and even a knitting whisperer. I was turning into the Mark Walberg of a new Antiques Knitting Roadshow.

THE MUSEUM

THE KNITTING TOUR DIDN'T GIVE us much time to sightsee, but Tex and I could not leave Winnipeg without visiting the new Canadian Museum for Human Rights, which had opened eight months earlier. It is the only national museum built in Canada since 1967, and the first museum with a national scope to be built outside Ottawa.

What better place to build a monument to our humanity than Winnipeg, where the streets expose Canada's history of injustice, where the bricks and mortar attest to human grit and fortitude, and where the Forks, the point where the waters of the Assiniboine from the west join the Red River from the south, has provided a place for humans to gather for at least six thousand years.

Given the location's contested history, it should come as no surprise that the creation of the museum was laden with controversy over partnerships, personalities and politics, in addition to its treatment of First Nations issues. It isn't a simple thing to build a monument that celebrates our humanity and bears witness to our inhumanity as well.

Some Canadians bristle at the thought that our country is anything but a good guy. In many respects, compared to our neighbour down south, we are pretty good. We didn't have the outright massacres that occurred during the new-comers' incursion into the American West. Our revolution doesn't amount to much when juxtaposed with the American Revolution or the Civil War. But our good-guy reputation has also hindered the search for our real identity. Only recently have we begun to cut through our patina of nice and realize that there is more to this country. We are finally opening up about Canada's childhood secrets and acknowledging both the light and dark sides of our history.

You might be thinking this topic is a bit heavy for a knitting road trip. But the main story I share in my workshops about the Coast Salish knitters mirrors many of the stories told in the Canadian Museum for Human Rights. The knitters were innovative, creative and adaptive women who fused their weaving skills, their tools, their techniques and their artistry with new ideas about spinning, weaving and yarn to make the sweater that became known as a Cowichan. The sweater became a British Columbia icon and a marketing sensation. Yet it wasn't the knitters who got rich. They were paid a pittance for their back-breaking work and were subjected to social alienation, racism and oppressive business practices. In spite of it all, they still loved to knit. They were proud they could provide for their families but resented that the same people who loved their sweaters did not accept the knitters themselves as equals.

This is not just a Canadian story. Knitters in Central and South America, Europe and Asia have worked under the same conditions and experienced the same ambivalent relationship to their vocation.

The bright side is that in every workshop on my knitting tour I met Canadians who wanted to be part of creating a better relationship with Indigenous people and new immigrants. The knitters brought their sweaters—bona fide Cowichans, Cowichan look-alikes, White Buffalo sweaters and Mary Maxims—because they wanted to connect with their Canadian identity and understand more about the troubling cultural issues in our country. I analyzed their sweaters and told them the stories found in the stitches— knitting techniques the Coast Salish established and those they borrowed from European settlers. We talked about the borrowing and sharing that continues as Coast Salish knitters copy White Buffalo patterns, which were themselves inspired by earlier Coast Salish sweaters, which were copied stitch-by-stitch from European knitting they pulled apart— the never-ending cycle of creation.

There are still some fashion designers who falsely call their sweaters Cowichan or Siwash, but I didn't meet those people on the road. My knitting workshops were places to talk about how honour intersects with cultural appropriation. Sweaters can represent a true fusion of cultures, and both knitting your own sweaters and wearing other people's knitting can be an act of respect and reconciliation.

OH CANADA

AN ODE TO THE MUSEUM OF HUMAN RIGHTS

Red dresses hang in a misty forest diorama
A little girl presses her nose against the glass
Mommy, what does it mean?
The dresses remind us that there are girls who have
    never been found

Trees shimmer to the pulse of the paddles of an-
    cient mighty mixed bloods
hauling goods to deep forest places
great open spaces
bringing old Europe to new possibilities
curious entrepreneurs wait in Cree villages
cautiously thinking ahead
never imagining what would come of the simple
    exchange
a beaver pelt for a cast iron fry pan

Oh Canada
I am a witness wrapped in pieces of the past
in remnants of a blanket
patched together by thread
once tenuous and frayed
now strong enough to fasten
an old shoe with a curled toe

left in the schoolyard
the ankle and calf of an invisible boy
with tousled hair
still twisted

Crushed bricks from the old school buildings
make mortar
binding the sons and daughters of this great
    Canada
We aren't children anymore
we are growing ourselves up
we know our mommas and papas weren't perfect
they had their nasty side
no more games of pretend
now we face it
we can change it

Oh Canada
The alabaster path into the sun
once bearing precious ointment to heal the healer
to anoint the anointed
I linger to draw the warmth into my skin
I step weightlessly

I get it, Canada
we don't have to be good guys to be good guys
Let's just be real

We can do this thing

Our sons and daughters expose naked truths
And write new stories
with new tunes

Oh Canada
I am going to sing their songs of possibility

THIRD TRY

BY THE TIME WE LEFT Winnipeg I had knit about ten inches on the green version of my Canadian dress. But over the last three or four inches I had had a looming feeling designers know well: this is not going to turn out. Before I knit another stitch, I needed to conduct a brutally honest evaluation.

After drawing several variations of the maple leaf for my design, I had settled on a large leaf motif that I intertwined—one right side up, the other upside down—in an Escher-like pattern. I thought bold sections of green would look striking against the random stripes of grey I imagined for the background.

What I hadn't considered was that the leaves formed large blocks of a single colour, sometimes up to twenty stitches at a time, with no detailing in a second colour to interrupt them. This had presented me with a colourwork challenge: should I proceed intarsia style, a method where I would need to use many separate bobbins of green yarn, that becomes even more complicated when working in the round, or should I continue with the long blocks and give up the elasticity?

There are pros and cons to both approaches. Intarsia is a nuisance to knit—you are constantly untangling the balls of design colour. And even if I was willing to brave using eight or ten bobbins, the complexity of the intertwined maple-leaf design meant there would be many rounds where intarsia was confusing and unnecessary.

I had decided to carry the unused yarn over the large sections of single colour. But even if I could have carried it without it showing on the front side, I had a stretch issue. I maintain that Coast Salish colourwork produces maximum elasticity, but only when you are changing colours every few stitches.

I pulled the dress out of my knitting bag and flattened it over my knees. I examined the stitches. They had the unevenness that comes with long sections of a single colour, and while I don't mind the background colour showing through to some degree, this was pushing my limit. That being said, I was willing to trade off some background colour showing in order to achieve maximum stretchiness. I pulled the knitting lengthwise and widthwise. I simulated sitting and kneeling and imagined the dress extending over my bum.

My feeling was right. This was not turning out well.

I put the knitted piece on the dashboard to get the road-trip version of standing back. The bold green maple leaves I had thought would please Escher now looked more like something found in a kids' colouring book. I pulled the visor down and held the knitted section up to the mirror to get a sense of what the dress would look like reflected back.

Tex glanced over. "Don't tell me."

"Shhh."

"I know what you're up to."

"Seriously. Please. Shhh. I need a few minutes in silence to examine the relationships that are forming in my dress."

"Oh, for gawd sakes."

Designing knitwear is a process of choreographing colour, shapes, techniques and materials to create a tangible expression of the imagination. It's performance art. My endgame is to achieve harmony among all the components and, most importantly, to feel my own sense of pleasure and peace. At the same time, I don't want to lull observers to sleep. I want to make a statement, to communicate something that makes people pause in their looking long enough to remember what they've seen. My maple-leaf dress was afflicted by internal dissonance. It was out of sync with itself.

"Don't do it," Tex warned. His face darkened, and he shot me the kind of look his Viking ancestors must have used when threatening their opponents. "Just don't do it. I mean it, Sylvia."

I had already begun to pull the stitches off the needle.

"Give that to me. I'll do something with it."

"No, you won't. This"—I held it up for one last time— "will cease to exist."

Some designers knit mini-versions of their design ideas until they get it right, then make a life-size creation. If I could make the conceptual leap from doll size to my size, it would save me a lot of time. But while I can visualize how something will look, I cannot visualize how it will function. I need to put it on, or put it on someone else. I need to wear it around.

"I already know that I don't want to wear it."

Tex gripped the steering wheel to prevent his hands from jabbing out and snatching the disappearing maple leaves.

All he could do was say, "Sometimes I don't understand you."

ONTARIO

TEX'S COUNTRY

ASK ANY CROSS-CANADA ROAD TRIPPERS, and they will tell you that the journey from the Manitoba/Ontario border to Sault Ste. Marie is both one of the most beautiful and one of the most daunting stretches of the country. The 1,200 kilometres through northern Ontario and over the hump on the north side of Lake Superior represent almost one-quarter of the entire distance across the country. It's twice as far as driving across Germany or France, with fewer gas stations, hotels and restaurants than you will find in most small Canadian towns.

We were prepared. The cooler was packed with food and drinks, an audiobook was at the ready and Tex filled the tank with fuel in Kenora. We were heading into maple-leaf country, so I had a pencil, an eraser and some graph paper on my lap. I was ready to be inspired. However, my head-down-to-work approach wasn't what Tex had in mind.

"You won't be able to draw that complicated design on this road. It winds too much, and you'll miss the best scenery."

I've always been dubious about scenery and sightseeing as concepts. Both words make me think of people with leaflets in hand, traipsing from one overrated destination to the next. At the end of the day they collapse in their hotel rooms, tend to the blisters on their feet and talk about how wonderful all the sights were while secretly pondering why the hell they didn't just lie down on a park bench and go to sleep.

The word "scenery" makes it sound as if the primary purpose of waterfalls, coastlines and cliffs is to be seen, as if the natural world is a museum or an art gallery. Awe-inspiring landscapes become fodder for photos.

Road tripping makes sightseeing an even less engaged pastime. In comfortable cars on well-tended highways, we whizz by natural spectacles with a nod or an "ah" at the most. As long as the audiobook is good and my knitting is complicated, I am worse than a passive sightseer: I can end up missing the sights and scenery altogether.

Tex was not going to let that happen. He had already driven this stretch of road twenty times that he could remember, and the day's drive around the lake is one of his favourite stretches of highway in the country. Tex doesn't sightsee; he's the tour guide. He has been on the road for more than fifty years. His work teaching energy-efficient building practices and technology has taken him to every important and not-so-important city in Canada and more than 130 First Nations. He doesn't just fly in or drive through; he listens to the people. He investigates and interrogates the landscape.

Tex is essentially settler-Canadian, a prototypical Ontarian, one of the solid, smart, tough people on whose watch fields were cleared, stumps were hauled and crops were planted. He can tell you the names of all the prime ministers, along with their claims to fame, their foibles and the missteps that took them down.

We were heading into Tex's territory, and the next two days were filled with a series of "did you know?" comments. I discovered that I didn't know much about Ontario, and it seemed as if Tex knew everything. What he didn't know we Googled when we got to our hotel.

Just east of Winnipeg, we crossed the southern border of Canada's boreal forest.

"The boreal forest had marginal land for agriculture, so settlers didn't like it much," Tex informed me. "It covers about 65 per cent of Canada, and something like five hundred or six hundred Indigenous communities—Cree, Dene, Anishinaabe, Métis—are in the boreal belt—great hunting and trapping land. Most of the region is still relatively free of industry, although development is pushing its way up from the south. Mining always has its sights set on expanding north." He glanced over at me. "Most people think of the boreal forest as ancient wilderness. It might be ancient in the sense that every square kilometre hasn't been traipsed on by people, but did you know that insects, forest fires and weather play havoc with the trees here, so they have a shorter life cycle than trees in the forests out west? Did you know that's why western forests are so much taller? They have longer to grow before nature takes them out."

No, I had no idea.

"It's like your hair," Tex continued. "Some people have long hair cycles and some people have short hair cycles. You know how some people's hair grows really long, and other people's hair just won't get that long no matter how hard they try to grow it?"

No, I had no idea. These are the sort of "facts" that are hard to confirm on the Internet. But I felt an affinity with the scrubby boreal forest. I must have a very short hair cycle, because I can only dream about growing a lush head of long, thick hair.

The boreal forest cuts a swath across the country, from the Yukon and northern British Columbia to Newfoundland

and Labrador. It is part of the boreal zone that forms a ring around the North Pole just south of the Arctic Circle in countries such as Norway, Sweden, Russia and China, taking up 33 per cent of the earth's forested area and 14 per cent of the earth's land. Alaska's and Canada's boreal forests cover 1.5 billion acres, a region larger than India.

Fifty-five per cent of Canada's land mass is made up of this forest. Pine, spruce, larch, fir, poplar and birch populate the space between the treeless tundra and the temperate zone in southern Canada. The area contains thousands of lakes, rivers and wetlands. It contains more unfrozen fresh water than any other ecosystem in the world and is home to half the bird species in the country.

"You'd think Canada would have some kind of coordinated approach to this region. But it doesn't seem to capture the politicians' attention," Tex said with a shrug.

Lake Superior was also the closest thing to an ocean I would see for another three weeks, something a West Coaster notices. It is, by surface area, the world's largest freshwater lake, holding more water than all the other Great Lakes combined. In fact, Lake Superior contains 10 per cent of the earth's fresh surface water. It has almost 3,000 kilometres of shoreline and is 260 kilometres across at its widest part.

"Did you know that this lake has enough water in it to flood North and South America to a depth of thirty centimetres?" Tex asked. "And it's old water. It takes an average of two hundred years for a drop of water from the lake to find its way to the St. Lawrence River and out to the ocean."

"Wow. No wonder it's called Lake Superior."

"Not really. It became known as Superior in the seventeenth century. French explorers called it *le lac superieur*, which just means 'Upper Lake,' or the lake north of Lake Huron."

Henry Wadsworth Longfellow borrowed the Ojibwe word *gichigami*, loosely meaning "big sea" or "huge water," for his poem "The Song of Hiawatha":

> *By the shores of Gitche Gumee,*
> *By the shining Big-Sea-Water . . .*

Gordon Lightfoot immortalized the lake in his song "The Wreck of the *Edmund Fitzgerald*," which commemorated the loss of the twenty-nine crew members who sank with their boat to the bottom of the lake, never to be seen again.

The ancient rift valley beneath the waters of Lake Superior began with iron-rich deposits dating back 1.5 billion years, when the area was a desert. Layered on top is sedimentary and volcanic rock—part of the Canadian Shield, the geological core of North America. Glaciers gouged deep into the earth as they left the great basin, forming Lake Superior. The region's rocks are riddled with fractures and soft eroding minerals, meaning the banks at the roadside expose the earth's ancient stories.

We pulled over just outside Nipigon to examine the impressive layers of red rocks.

"This is one of my favourite parts of the region," Tex said. "You can see the earth's earliest history. I always think it's sort of apropos that it looks rusty."

I remembered the story we had learned in school about Canada's early roots as a trading country. In the spring, as soon as the ice broke, voyageurs from Montreal would navigate their birchbark freight canoes, laden with European goods, along the rivers leading to the shores of Lake Superior. They paddled the north shore of the lake to Fort William, now Thunder Bay, and then down the rivers heading west. At the same time, men from the trading posts in the west and the north filled their canoes with pelts from Indigenous trappers and headed east and south. The two groups rendezvoused at Fort Frances, where they made their business deals and partied, but they had little time to relax. They soon had to repack their canoes and hit the road, so to speak—Canada's first long-haul truckers. The early onset of the northern winter gave them only enough time to get home before the ice returned. Those were hard days in the North, and although Canadians are not much given to celebrating homegrown heroes, these hardy men were as close to superstars as it gets.

Deal Breaker

I LEARNED TO KNIT WHEN I was a young girl, and by the time I started dating I knit all the time. Whenever my boyfriend and I watched TV, I would knit—I can't sit in front of a TV without doing something with my hands. It took me a while to realize it annoyed him, and finally he asked me not to knit while we were watching TV together. That was the end of that boyfriend. The next fellow I dated bought me a set of needles the first Christmas we spent together. I married him, and we still watch TV together, me with my knitting, him with his beer, happily ever after.

GROUPIES

WHEN I FIRST ASKED TEX if he would like to go on a cross-Canada knitting road trip, he said he had always thought about getting his old band together and touring. A few of the musicians from his old bands, Wingspan, Bachus and Air, were still playing music, and Tex can still sing some pretty formidable Rod Stewart, Mick Jagger and Neil Young. His groups had been relatively good in their day. Air's claim to fame was winning CHUM radio's 1969 Battle of the Bands in Toronto, beating out the band that later became Rush. Tex didn't have big dreams for his band reunion. He thought maybe they could perform a few gigs in southern Ontario, where they had once played bars and dance halls. A knitting road trip? That had never occurred to him.

As we crossed the border into Ontario, Tex admitted that while his old band might have attracted more men than a knitting tour would, our tour was certainly attracting more women.

"They are the same beautiful women who would have been dancing at our gigs in the '70s," he mused. "Now here they are with their knitting needles."

DETOUR

OUR TOUR WENT THROUGH SEVERAL stages of planning. At the comfortable stage, the ratio of workshop, travel and rest days left Tex and me plenty of time to make spontaneous choices on the road. The next stage came with a warning from Diane that there was no room for spur-of-the-moment detours. As word of our travelling knitting-and-storytime show spread on social media, calls came pouring in, and Diane filled in so many "rest days" there was no more wiggle room.

Tex and I had looked over the itinerary in Winnipeg.

"It's tight, but we can do it. Even if someone cancels," we told Diane, "this is cut-off time." We all agreed to that. Then another call came in.

"We read about the knitting tour, and we have a story we want to tell. We'd like Sylvia and Tex to come to Sioux Lookout. There is a group of knitters up here who knit baby hats, and we would love a workshop," a woman explained.

Diane phoned us. "I have never even heard of a place called Sioux Lookout," she said.

Tex had. He had been there many times. "Syl, you are going to want to visit this place," he told me. "It sounds like they have a great story, and if you are going to understand the North, you really need to go to Sioux Lookout."

Sioux Lookout would be a one-hour diversion off the Trans-Canada, up Highway 72.

"That stretch is already long enough," I protested. "Do we really need to give it a whole extra day?"

"Yes," Tex insisted. "In the end you will be happy we did."

SIOUX LOOKOUT IS A LITTLE town of about five thousand with a uniquely optimistic feel to it. On the road into town we passed a lake that lay smooth and silvery in the sun and was hemmed in with a white sandy beach and green playgrounds. Speedboats and seaplanes were moored to the docks that jutted out from the lakeshore. It was a quiet weekday in late May. The town appeared to be waiting for summer to arrive.

Although it is well off the beaten track, Sioux Lookout appears, to an outsider, to be quintessential Ontario cottage country. But there is more to it than that. It is a major transportation/service hub for northern Ontario communities, many of which only have winter roads. Flights from Winnipeg and Thunder Bay bring people to Sioux Lookout, where they then board smaller planes that take them to the twenty-nine inland communities of the James Bay lowlands. The villages, which were once known by names given to them by the Hudson's Bay Company or federal agents, such as Lansdowne House, Big Trout Lake and Osnaburgh House, are now known as Neskantaga, Kitchenuhmaykoosib Inninuwug and Mishkeegogamang.

The new names, which I couldn't pronounce, made me think of a common saying these days among First Nations people: "No decisions about Indians without Indians." The quote is attributed to Jules Sioui, a Wendake activist from Quebec during the 1940s. In his testimony to the first national hearings on the Indian Act in 1947, Sioui attributed the appalling living conditions in Indigenous communities in part to the fact that Indigenous people had no governing control over their own lives. He believed that Indigenous people should be included in every decision government made about them. It has taken decades, but we are witnessing Sioui's influence in the movement by First Nations across the country to rid their communities of names imposed on them by governments, monarchs and businessmen, and to officially change these to names of their own choosing from their languages.

Names were just the start of the movement. Indigenous languages that we once thought were extinct are now being spoken by children in every First Nations community across Canada. Several of my grandchildren are learning their Indigenous language, SENĆOŦEN, a dialect of the Coast Salishan language, at their local public schools. All except Ella, who is in SENĆOŦEN immersion at ȽÁU,WELṈEW̱ Tribal School. I know things have fundamentally changed in my country when I eavesdrop on her talking to her dolls in SENĆOŦEN or hear her singing to herself in the bath in her Indigenous language.

We drove through town and up the hill to the airport. Tex said we had to go there. "It's where you will see what makes this town tick."

Inside, the waiting room was buzzing. Indigenous people with bags full of groceries and household items were visiting with old friends from neighbouring communities while waiting for their flights. One man had two large bags of takeout chicken and a box of doughnuts—treats he couldn't get at home. I was beginning to understand: Sioux Lookout is a modern rendezvous, and airlines like

Air Creebec, Wasaya Airways and Bearskin Airlines are the new transport canoes.

The knitting group we were visiting was made up of doctors, nurses and other hospital staff, so we headed across town to find the Meno Ya Win Health Centre. We were awestruck when we got there. A giant drum looms over the hostel where families can stay when their loved ones are in hospital. Inside, comfortable chairs encircle a grand central fireplace. Towering cedar poles form a longhouse-style roof structure, and curved beams look like giant canoes hanging from the ceilings of the halls. This is a hospital unlike any I've seen, and it is not just an architectural accomplishment. Meno Ya Win is Canada's foremost medical facility serving Indigenous communities, fusing modern and traditional practices. We later learned that there had originally been two hospitals in Sioux Lookout: the Sioux Lookout Indian Hospital (later renamed the Sioux Lookout Zone Hospital) for Indigenous people, which provided vastly substandard medical services, and the Sioux Lookout General Hospital for everyone else. Both hospitals were torn down in the early 2000s, and Meno Ya Win opened its door to everyone in 2010.

Do I dare question Shakespeare's wisdom that a name is just a name and "that which we call a rose by any other name would smell as sweet"? I was beginning to understand that names are a significant part of a new story about Canada. It was not a small thing when the "Indian" and "General" hospitals were combined into one, which was called Meno Ya Win, meaning "a state of mental, emotional, physical and spiritual wellness"—for everyone.

BABY HATS

PEGGY SANDERS WAS THE PERSON behind our visit to Sioux Lookout, so it made sense that we didn't start the workshop until she arrived. Peggy was one of Sioux Lookout's most distinguished and beloved citizens. She came to the town as a teacher in 1944, when she was eighteen. She had intended to stay for only a couple of years, but then she got married and had three babies and stayed until her death in 2017.

It's safe to say that Peggy dedicated her life to making Sioux Lookout the sort of town she wanted for her children. She was instrumental in establishing the museum and making it a success. She championed literacy by founding the town's first public library. She was also a founding member of the local anti-racism committee, with its slogan "Together We Are Better." She was named to the Order of Canada in 2006 for her work building relationships between Indigenous and non-Indigenous communities.

When Peggy arrived, shortly after the others, she pulled out her needles and eyed the toque kit that lay on the table.

"Back in the day," Peggy told us, "and still today when First Nations moms from the North need a hospital, they are flown to Sioux Lookout to give birth to their babies. Sometimes they only stay a few days, but usually they stay a few weeks. Sometimes, if there are complications, the mom will come to town months before the birth. Most of these moms leave other children at home. It's terribly disruptive for their families. They used to be in the federal hospital, all alone. I worried about them, so I went up to the hospital to visit them. Pretty soon I got to know some of them. And over the years I got to know the children who had been born. After a while I found myself visiting these babies, all grown up, now in the hospital having babies of their own. I wanted to reach out and make a connection between the northern people and Sioux Lookout. I wanted them to feel comfortable.

"I started knitting baby hats so that when the mom and baby went home, they took with them something loving and warm. I don't know how many I've knit. My goal was to send every baby born in Sioux Lookout home to the North in a hand-knitted hat. I also started making hats for the preemies who had to stay in the hospital when their mothers returned home to look after their other children. And the tiniest hats of all, the size of oranges, for the stillborn.

"This wonderful group of knitters, they call themselves the Northern Knitters, took hold of the idea and started knitting hats as well.

"My eyes aren't what they used be," she said, setting the knitting kit aside. "I'm just happy to be here."

In 2012, the centennial year for Sioux Lookout, the Northern Knitters had committed to knitting a hat for every baby born in the hospital, making Peggy's long-time dream come true. That meant they had to knit five hundred hats. They did it! And they did it again the following year, and the one after that. A wall in the hospital is covered with photos of smiling parents holding newborns wearing Northern Knitters hats.

Peggy said the hats are now a multi-generational thing—mothers and fathers told her about adding their baby's hat to the hats their own parents received when their children were born. She told us that one day an excited young man came up to her in the grocery store and said, "I still have the baby hat you knitted for me when I was born. We're expecting, and I'm looking forward to getting a new hat for my son. Thank you!"

When we got to Thunder Bay, I bought some machine-washable merino wool in grey and white. I knit six tiny hats, none of them bigger than preemie size. I knit one special hat that was even smaller, for a stillborn, in memory of the baby I never got to bring home from the hospital forty years ago.

When we reached Huntsville, I packaged up the hats and sent them off to the Northern Knitters.

YARN STORES

ON THE ROAD THERE WERE no Monday mornings, Friday nights or weekends. One day of the week was the same as the next. Even so, when we arrived for a workshop at Threads in Time, in a rundown building on a deserted main street in Thunder Bay's inner city, I thought we'd made a mistake. It was 9:45 on a Sunday morning.

The owner, Lynn, met us at the door with a hug. She had pushed the wool bins and display cases aside to make space at the back of her store. All the chairs were filled with knitters drinking coffee and chatting. Their knitting bags were stuffed under their seats, and they were each working on a project. There was no mistake; we were playing to a sold-out crowd.

"Something's going on here that I haven't thought about before," I said to Tex afterward, as we were packing up. "These yarn shops are different from other stores. They are more like businesses-turned-clubhouses. Retail shops-turned-living rooms."

It was an observation I'd make again and again as our tour continued. In some cases, the yarn shops were literally spaces eked out of private homes. In Vernon, Camella had renovated her family home to give the main floor over to A Twist of Yarn. In Sioux Lookout, knitters were anxiously waiting for their yarn shop to reopen. The shop was in a basement room in the owner's house and only open half the year because the owner lived away the rest of the time.

It wasn't just the locations that made yarn shops feel like living rooms, either. I got the same feeling of belonging at Wet Coast Wool in Vancouver, where the street noise made it hard for us to hear each other speak, and in the out-of-the-way Saskatoon industrial district where we found Prairie Lily Knitting.

Each yarn shop is unique, and in each place the workshop had a different dynamic. The Purple Sock in Coldwater, a beautiful little nineteenth-century Ontario mill town, is in a historic building surrounded by classy novelty stores that appeal to sophisticated shoppers coming from suburbia to look for something special. The walls of The Purple Sock were lined with cubbies stuffed with rainbows of yarn. The owner, another Lynn, had placed a tight circle of chairs around the main room in her shop, making it feel like we were at a private club and draped in an exquisite blanket.

At Eliza's Buttons and Yarn in Barrie, we met after closing time in a typical '90s mall surrounded by utilitarian offices selling real estate and insurance. The room was grey and square, with a stark, box-store feel to it that softened when we met Elizabeth. She graciously served coffee as she worked the room, making everyone comfortable. She had sold all the spots for the knitting part of my workshop but made arrangements for people who just wanted to come hear the stories: they sat in a semicircle around the outside of the knitters, with a journalist from the Barrie newspaper who had also come to listen. The evening ended up being half knitting workshop/half house party.

We found Creative Yarns in an uninteresting '60s strip mall on a busy thoroughfare in Scarborough, at the centre of Canada's suburban concrete jungle. Tex and I sat in the van eating Armenian pizza and a Portuguese sweet roll, wondering how anyone could turn such a bleak location into a home for knitting. When we opened the shop's front door, we got the answer. The place was more like a trendy art gallery than a yarn shop. Quirky, colourful and sophisticated knitted garments crowded the yarn-filled room. Many of the pieces hanging throughout the store were creations of the owner, Nina; others were samples from published patterns. Sitting on two overstuffed sofas around a table covered with plates of cookies and teacups, four women were deep in conversation. Two of them were talking about someone's troubled daughter, who had run off with an older man. The other two were huddled together troubleshooting a knitting pattern.

After we'd spent two days at Creative Yarns, Tex said to me, "Why would those women ever want to go home?"

Owning a yarn store is a dream that is shared by many. My ten-year-old grandson, Joseph, wants to run our family knitting business when he grows up. He intends to operate it out of the family home in WJOŁEŁP. We dream together about adding a sweater museum to satisfy my interest as a sweater historian. He has ideas of how the shop will look, where the cars can be parked and the sign he will put at the end of the road.

The yarn stores we visited were someone's dream. Upon revisiting several of the shops since our tour I've found some have closed their doors, others have renamed and rebranded, while most are still thriving and fulfilling their creators' dreams.

The Yarn Business

WE ALL KNEW THAT LIL [not her real name] needed a holiday. She had had some health challenges, and she was getting burned out. But we knew she would never take a real break. She doesn't make enough in the shop to hire someone to take her place and let her get away. So a bunch of us got together and told her we had booked her a hotel room for a whole week. We told her it was paid for, so she couldn't cancel. We organized a schedule to keep the shop open. One woman knew the business side of things, and the rest of us came in to serve customers. We took care of everything. We even went over to Lil's place to help her pack her suitcase.

THIS SHOP USED TO BE run by Linda [not her real name] and her husband. He was a wonderful man. He knew all about everything, and he was such a gracious host; he'd greet you with a cup of tea. A year and a half ago he died suddenly. It was an awful blow. No one knew if Linda would be able to go it alone. A group of us customers got together and did our own crowdsourcing to help her through the worst of it. Some of us volunteered in the shop, and we made sure that things were covered. Now that she's back on her feet, we're still here for her if she needs us.

YARN SHOPS ARE NOT MONEY-MAKERS, especially in a small town like this. I guess you could figure that out yourself. But it's my dream job. I had to sell my house and move into my parents' basement suite in order to fund it. I'm making it work. I can't afford much staff, so I'm pretty well here all the time, but it's like my home so I don't mind. My customers are my friends. I get into the best conversations. I bring in workshops like yours so we all keep learning. Is there a better life?

—◯—

I GOT INTO THIS BUSINESS for exactly the reason everyone will tell you is wrong, wrong, wrong. I wanted to have access to all the best yarn. I wanted my own private stash of all the fibres I had ever dreamed of. So how's it going? That part of it has been a success. I get all the yarn I want. The business end is a struggle, just like people warned. Don't get into this business if you want to get rich without working very hard. But if you want an amazing community, if you want to immerse yourself in the creative side of things, if you want to get to know really interesting, good people, and if you love your shop—because you are going to spend a lot of time in it—then this is the business for you. You get to hang out with yarn all day, and who doesn't want to do that?

KNITTING GOES RUNWAY

WEARING KNIT FUR, LUXURIOUS BEAVER inside and out, is like bathing in feathers. Knit fur is the Rolls-Royce, the Jaguar, the Bentley of knitting, and it was first designed and produced by Canada's own Paula Lishman. What could be more Canadian than knit beaver? The little animal whose pelts drew European traders to this part of the world and put Canada on the map, the little animal that almost became extinct because the world couldn't get enough of its fur, is back. There are as many beaver in Canada today as there were before the beaver trade began, and Paula Lishman has invented a new way to honour Canada's national animal.

We visited Paula in her workshop in the basement of a clothing store in the historic section of Port Perry, Ontario, a tourist destination northeast of Toronto. Now mostly retired, with her business vastly reduced, she showed us the custom orders she was designing and introduced us to the lone sewer who was putting the designs together.

Paula's knit fur was once a multi-million-dollar New York runway fashion success. At six foot three, Paula was her own best model. She has been named a Canadian Woman Entrepreneur of the Year, and been featured in magazines like *Chatelaine* and *Canadian Business*. But ask her to describe perfect happiness and she will likely say something about family and sitting in a comfortable chair with knitting or crocheting on her lap. In spite of her star status, knitting is her obsession. She often took her knitting on plane trips to New York, making shawls and wraps on the way to and from shows.

Paula was born in Montreal and grew up in Goose Bay, Labrador, where she became passionate about the necessity of fur. While trapping can be exploitative, it is also a traditional activity that, done right, is sustainable. Paula buys her pelts from Algonquin trappers in northern Ontario and Quebec, where trapping is an indispensable part of life. The Algonquin have a visceral respect for the animals they trap and the territory that sustains them.

"It was trappers," Paula reminds us, "who blew the whistle on acid rain."

She has the pelts dyed, stretched and trimmed by hand; every guard hair is plucked. "If the straight hairs that shed water get into any of your garments, you feel it. They stick right into you," she explains. Paula cuts the pelts into narrow strips and spins the fur with cotton yarn for strength. She employs hand and machine knitters to produce sumptuous, one-of-a-kind hats, scarfs, shawls and jackets.

In the mid-1990s, at the height of her business, Paula employed almost two hundred people from the rural area around Port Perry. These days she is not the only one in the business of making knit fur, although her designs are still sought after around the world.

Paula has been an important voice in a new narrative about the fur business. She argues that Indigenous people have a way of honouring animals while trapping them and wearing their skins, and she says that it is possible for the rest of us to learn from the Algonquin trappers and rebuild our relationships with the natural world.

"Keep the trappers on the land," she advises. "They know how to trap in a sustainable way. Not everyone sees it this way, and they are entitled to their own opinions. I feel that I am honouring the life of the animal. Wearing beaver is organic, renewable, long-lasting and biodegradable. It's naturally Canadian."

The more I learn about the destructive qualities of synthetics, especially fleece, the more the new narrative about fur makes sense to me. I am increasingly convinced that it is artificial fibres we should be worried about.

While I had never worn fur before, once I heard Paula's story and saw photos of her apparel, I was interested. After I touched knit fur, stretched it, draped it, put a hat on my head, wrapped a shawl around my shoulders and swathed myself in a cape, I experienced an embryonic feeling that let me know I was deeply in touch with something real.

I bought a raspberry-coloured short jacket from Paula for a very good price. When I'm wearing it and someone hugs me, they often hold on for a few extra seconds. I can feel their fingers sink into the fur. I can sense their curiosity.

"What is that?" they ask.

When I tell them, they look sheepish and ask, "Can I touch it again?"

THE OTHER ICON

***

THE COLOURS HAVE FADED, AND the whites have bronzed with age. Unravelled knots have turned into small holes that could easily be fixed with a darning needle and a length of yarn. Other than that, the old Mary Maxim sweaters in my collection could likely hold up to hard wear for another fifty or sixty years, thanks to the sturdy Canadian wool that seems to take almost as long to wear in as to wear out.

Mary Maxim is the "other" iconic Canadian sweater. Its roots date back to the early 1950s in Sifton, Manitoba, where Sifton Wool Products, a mail-order company run by Willard and Olive McPhedrain, started selling knitting kits. Their bulky sweater designs were inspired partly by the motifs found on Coast Salish sweaters and partly by the imagination of Mary Maxim designers like Bill King, who created knitting motifs with all things Canadiana, from moose, geese and giant salmon to hockey, curling and the Royal Canadian Mounted Police, with Disney characters thrown in for good measure.

Knitters told stories about perusing Mary Maxim catalogues to find exactly the right kit to fit the interests of the wearer, and about making customized sweaters—a pink ballerina for the aspiring dancer, a jumping horse for the equestrian.

The Mary Maxim store we were looking for appeared unexpectedly in the middle of farm country in southwestern Ontario, just outside Paris. We knew we were there when we saw what must be the biggest knitting needle in the country attached to a Mary Maxim sign.

I was surprised by the suburban-mall feel of the parking lot and storefront. I had expected something a little more stereotypically Canadian. A rustic log cabin perhaps? I opened the front door thinking we would be met by bins of natural wool and shelves of knitting kits. But these days Mary Maxim is a craft store, more like Michaels than a yarn shop. Except, as I overheard one shopper say, "The prices here aren't as cheap as Walmart."

At the far end of the store we located the knitting department, though it was almost impossible to find the sturdy wool that had lasted so long in the sweaters in my collection. Most of the yarn was acrylic or acrylic blend. Some patterns were slightly updated versions of sweaters from the '50s and '60s, although many of the motifs hadn't changed. You can still get patterns with apples or cowboy hats or grizzly bears to knit on your sweater.

I bought a kit that was similar to the 2010 Winter Olympics sweater design. The synthetic yarn felt too much like plastic to be Canadian, and I was guessing that when I got around to knitting the sweater, it wouldn't be in anyone's collection in sixty years.

My pilgrimage to Mary Maxim was a disappointment. I didn't discover a treasure trove of Canadian woolens. Instead of taking the Canadian classic in a new and interesting direction, Mary Maxim had shipped the whole thing offshore. The result was the same old designs packaged with imported substandard Chinese yarns. It appeared to be a missed opportunity.

However, I left the store with some conclusions regarding what sweaters were saying about being Canadian. While the motifs on Coast Salish sweaters did inspire the

McPhedrains when they launched their knitting kit business, Mary Maxim sweaters are not Cowichan knock-offs. Other than a few similar motifs and their bulky characteristics, the two sweaters don't have much in common. They feature very different construction methods, most easily seen in Mary Maxim's raglan sleeves, compared to the Cowichan drop sleeve. Mary Maxim designers created many of their own geometric patterns, often drawing on Argyle and Fair Isle knitting styles. Mary Maxim can claim to be the first to introduce large, lifelike designs that contain ballerinas, boats and golfers, and it was the first to take its patterns to such an intricate level, with huge graphs giving knitters stitch-by-stitch instructions to follow.

Over the years, Coast Salish knitters borrowed Mary Maxim designs to create large animal designs of their own. There is evidence that many Mary Maxim motifs became Coast Salish favourites. To my knowledge, Mary Maxim never sold a kit that was a direct copy of the structure of the Cowichan sweater, although the company gave some of its patterns names like "Iroquois" and "Chief's Sweater."

The study of Mary Maxim and Cowichan sweaters reinforces the idea that knitting is bigger than both of them. It is a borrowed skill, and it has been adapted and amended across the globe and down through time. It is truly a craft that belongs to us all.

Yet in the 1970s, when Cowichan sweaters became "the" thing to own, the polite borrowing of knitting techniques ran up against the harsh reality of commercial competition. The White Buffalo Company split off from Mary Maxim and developed a sweater intentionally designed to rival the Cowichan. White Buffalo developed a soft, natural-looking, six-strand yarn to resemble the bulky characteristics of Coast Salish handspun. The patterns followed Mary Maxim sweater construction, with raglan sleeves and sewn seams, but otherwise they aimed to reproduce Cowichan sweaters as closely as possible. Companies hired hand knitters, mostly women who were recent immigrants and willing to work for extremely low wages, to produce sweaters commercially from White Buffalo patterns. The White Buffalo products suppliers provided a one-stop marketing opportunity for Cowichan sweater shops, offering quantities of sweaters with standardized sizing, quality and designs, and eliminating the time-consuming process of buying one sweater at a time from individual Coast Salish knitters. Pretty soon, retail stores took copying Cowichan sweaters one step further. They sold Cowichan look-alikes next to the genuine sweaters, often calling the copies "Cowichans," undercutting the price and confusing consumers. Knitting had entered the era of rip-offs.

Coast Salish knitters fought unethical business practices, and the Cowichan Tribes attempted to prevent its name from being attached to the rip-offs. But they could not compete. By the early 1990s, bulky wool sweaters, similar to Cowichan sweaters, were also being imported from Central and South America, and staunching the flow was impossible.

While most of the knitters I met didn't know this story, they came to the workshops wanting to learn. They wanted to incorporate Cowichan designs and images as a way to honour that unique knitting tradition, in the same way they honour Fair Isle, Aran and Mary Maxim. These days Cowichan, Mary Maxim and White Buffalo are as Canadian as maple syrup and Tim Hortons, as is the story of borrowing, sharing and ripping off.

Pink Sweaters

I HAVE A SWEATER ETCHED in my memory. I know my grandmother knit it for me. I'm pretty sure it was a Mary Maxim pattern, but I've searched everywhere for it, and I can't find it in their archives. It was pink, and it had ballerinas doing pirouettes. It was my favourite sweater. I would do anything to be able to knit the same one for my granddaughter.

MY GRANDMA SAYS SHE KNIT sixteen Mary Maxim sweaters. Everyone in the family had one. They had moose, geese and golfers on them—you know the one with the fellow winding up to take a swing? My sweater was pink with clowns on the front and back. I wish I'd kept it. I loved that sweater. I remember feeling so proud whenever I wore it. I thought my grandmother was brilliant to be able to make those clowns out of wool. But when I think back, it must have been ghastly. We only have one photo of it, and it's pretty "out there." I don't think I'd let my daughter wear it. I doubt she'd wear it anyway. But in my heart it was so special.

ANOTHER OLDEST SWEATER

HEATHER HAD CONTACTED ME MONTHS before we left on our road trip after reading that I wanted to find the oldest sweater in the country.

"I'm not sure our sweater is the oldest," she wrote, "but it is my sister's family treasure, and it has an amazing story. You are going to want to come and see it."

We met Heather and Cris at their rural cottage just outside Port Perry. Serendipitously, Tex discovered the two of them were old friends he'd known years earlier.

The sweater lived with Heather's sister—the family-approved guardian of the treasure once owned by her father-in-law, a Japanese immigrant. Heather had had to persuade her sister that the sweater would be safe with her. She promised she would return it as soon as we had seen the special keepsake.

We learned that the sweater had belonged to a Japanese Canadian fisherman from Steveston, a historic salmon-canning centre at the mouth of the Fraser River, southwest of Vancouver. He had purchased the sweater from a Coast Salish knitter who had come from Vancouver Island to work in the cannery.

Like so many Japanese Canadian fishermen, the man was rounded up in 1942, when war broke out in the Pacific, on the suspicion that he was a threat to national security. The federal government confiscated his fishing boat, along with his property and personal effects—everything except his Cowichan sweater and the few meagre possessions he could fit into one small suitcase.

The man's family had dated the sweater back to the late 1930s. The yarn had been tightly spun and had held together for almost eighty years with hardly a frayed edge. The sweater body and sleeves had multiple bands of nondescript designs outlining the central band of repetitive crab-like motifs.

Like the other old sweaters we met on the road, this one used all the knitting techniques that have come to be associated with Coast Salish knitting, including beautiful over-and-under colourwork, drop sleeves and a three-piece knit-on collar. More importantly, the Japanese Canadian owner of the sweater had likely chosen it as one of his prize possessions because of its all-purpose practicality and durability. A good choice, given how many decades the sweater has survived.

The sweater is a treasure not only because of its significance to the family's history and its embodiment of the national experience of dispossession by Japanese Canadians during World War II, but also because it tells the story of the close relationship between the immigrants and Indigenous peoples of the West Coast. The two groups, both marginalized by the mainstream population before the war, came together on the fishing docks and in the thriving packing and canning industry along the BC coast. Heather's sister's sweater, like the one we saw at the Gilli-hook Heritage Knitters Guild in Calgary, made me wonder how many other Japanese Canadian families had Cowichan sweater stories to tell.

QUEBEC

MOTEL

I LOVE FRINGES ON ALMOST anything. Add beads, and the fringe just gets better. But there are boho fringed lampshades with cut-glass beads at high-end boutique hotels, and then there are faded fringed lampshades with plastic beads at 1970s motels in need of a retrofit.

We came across the second kind of fringe just past the Ontario border on our way to Montreal. Tex had made the room reservation based solely on location, which was not his usual practice. The motel hadn't received a good rating on Booking.com, but Tex knew we'd be arriving late, and there wasn't much to choose from. We got there after dark. A fabulously retro illuminated MOTEL sign out front beckoned us in from the highway.

I do a lot of travelling for work, and I have stayed in more hotels and motels than I can remember. Sleeping in a hotel room is like eating canned soup. There are different brands, but canned tomato soup is never anything but canned tomato soup. Even in the new Tetra Paks, it is still canned soup. You might find jarred tomato soup at a deli and think you can taste a difference, but even tomato soup in a fancy jar is canned tomato soup.

In the same way, motels and hotels have established what is essential. They know their customers do not want any surprises. Travellers willing to take a chance rent through Airbnb.

Road trips are like business trips. In my accommodations I'm not looking for an experience—I'm looking for a good sleep. I want white sheets (so I can check for bedbug residue) and a clean room with a neutral smell. (There is nothing more off-putting than a smell you can identify, whether it's a cleaning product, smoke, food or formaldehyde.) Although they are getting scarce, I like a bathtub. I prefer windows that open, as I've said, and I like the place to be a few years old or a few years post-renovation to give any off-gassing time to dissipate. In hotels, I like to see original art on the walls in the rooms and hallways. Original art disrupts the usual corporate hotel décor, and even if the pieces aren't local, they are at least a link to real human expression. An original painting or sculpture gets you close to homemade, or at least chef-made, tomato soup. And I'm a sucker for a good chocolate on the pillow.

I was tired and road-weary by the time we saw the flashing MOTEL sign. I waited in the van while Tex went to the reception office to get our key. He pressed the buzzer several times, making a sound as loud and familiar as the bells I remember from elementary school. Through the window I could see the owner rousing himself from a sleep in front of the TV, putting on his robe and slippers and walking through a door linking his living room to the motel.

Tex nosed the van right up to the door of our room. I jiggled the heavy metal key inside the lock until the door opened. I flipped on the light, took two steps and flopped on the bed. I lifted my head to examine the shiny, slippery, floral bedspread. It had worn through in several places, exposing stuffing like cotton candy.

A scattershot collection of faded, plastic-framed samplers and Norman Rockwell prints covered the turquoise walls. A tiny chrome-and-vinyl kitchen set sat in front of the window, chairs held together by duct tape, with a vase of plastic anemones for a centrepiece. The room was a perfect reconstruction of the 1950s, from the round kettle on the stove, the dial telephone and the glittery-tasselled sashes wrapped around the curtain rods, to the Gideon Bible in the side table.

Except the room was for real. For decades, travellers had fiddled with the lock and then rested between the flowered sheets under the slippery bedspread. The sagging threads on the beaded and fringed lampshade made me imagine the room had looked exactly the same for every one of us. The room was clean, and it didn't smell. Although the sheets weren't white, I dreamed well that night.

ROMANCE

POETS HAVE ALWAYS INTIMIDATED ME. I marvel at how they assemble seemingly random thoughts in such a way that love or fear or longing—mostly longing—oozes from the page and seeps into your veins, where it sometimes stays forever. I will never forget Pablo Neruda's sensual love poem about springtime and cherry trees. Or that E.E. Cummings wrote, "in Just-spring when the world is mud-luscious the little lame balloonman whistles far and wee." Those words are part of my soul. They come to me as easily as popular jingles.

I have always believed I am missing the stuff in the pit of my stomach that you need to write poetry, especially love poetry. It's not that I haven't fallen in love. I have experienced dripping, heart-wringing, exhausting longing that permeates everything. I have loved that person who refuses to stop breathing on me every waking and sleeping moment of my day, even though he is only in my imagination.

But I had never felt myself enough of a writer for love poetry until the first time I visited Quebec City alone, several years before our knitting tour. Then, like a lover searching for words, I scrambled to find things to say on the page other than *ahhh, ohhh, ummmm*.

Quebec City is Canada's Paris, our Copenhagen, our Florence. Grand old stone churches and tall-spired buildings nose up to the narrow streets. Cafés, boutiques, bakeries and art galleries line brick roads worn into grooves. Plaques date monuments back centuries and tell of battles and intrigues.

British Columbians, like me, have nothing to compare to the ancient architecture. The closest thing I've seen in the West is the Douglas fir tree on Meares Island near Tofino, BC, where a sign claims the tree was a seedling about the time Christopher Columbus found his way to North America.

To a British Columbian, Quebec City's age, its Frenchness and the deep-rooted presence of the Catholic Church make it feel more European than Canadian. But as a taxi driver there told me, "The French language is more Canadian than the English language. You westerners think this country is English, but it was French first. It was right here in Stadacona that Canada was first called Canada."

Of course he's right about the French/English thing. Other than the Viking presence on the East Coast a thousand years ago, and the Venetian John Cabot's brief encounter in the fifteenth century, French travellers Jacques Cartier, Pierre Du Gua de Monts and Samuel de Champlain were the first Europeans to visit what has become known as Canada. And as has been said, it was the French who adopted the Iroquois word *kanata* to refer to the village on the site of what became Quebec City. But the taxi driver ignored the fact that Canadians must incorporate the Indigenous peoples' prior claim to this country before any arguments between the French and English will be settled.

Quebec City is known as the "Gibraltar of the Americas" for its strategic importance. Atop Cap Diamant, overlooking the St. Lawrence River, sits the Citadelle de Quebec, Canada's oldest military installation. Adjoining it is the Plains of Abraham where, in September 1759, the famous battle between the armies of the British general Wolfe and the French general Montcalm was fought. These are places where the French, British, Indigenous people and Americans have shuffled allegiances and fought for control, with complicated results. The Americans were turned back. Indigenous people fought on all sides and ended up abandoned and decimated. The British won the battle, but the French retained their language, their culture and their way of life.

Perched on the hill now is the magnificent Chateau Frontenac, built as a Canadian Pacific Railway hotel in 1892. On the boardwalk in front of the hotel are benches overlooking the St. Lawrence. I sat and imagined I could feel the heartbeat of my country from its earliest colonial past to its sophisticated and hopeful present. I sensed the pulsating struggle between peoples vying for their piece of the territory and its wealth. I thought about my blithe assumption that the British had won and that part of the story was over. We hold on to our assumptions only when we haven't thought deeply enough about them. I was sitting at the heart of Canada's internal struggle, on the very place where the country was made. And the jostling is not over.

I could feel a new narrative arising in me. Quebec City is not European; it is Quebec. It is Canada. French is Canada's first immigrant language, but the multitudes of Indigenous languages are our first languages. English is this country's third language. The Iroquois were not destroyed. Like other First Peoples, they retreated, but now they are rebuilding and restoring their communities, languages and culture, and they are remaking Canada in the process.

Late one day, in a café in the old town, Tex and I befriended a young Quebecois man who talked about his province in a way that I, as a westerner, had never heard before.

"We have always had an attitude about the British, English Canada, what have you. They were the oppressors. We were the little kid brother, so to speak. We constantly felt like we needed to kick at their shins. But we grew up. What they call the Quiet Revolution of the 1960s built our economy and also cemented our sense of ourselves as a people. We don't have to prove ourselves to anyone. We live our culture, speak our language. We even have our own legal and government system. We own our province. The next generation isn't interested in fighting old battles. We don't want to waste our time. We are claiming what is ours and getting on with being a progressive, modern and very Quebec sort of place."

I hear similar words from my children, Adam, Joni and Heather. They are all Coast Salish leaders who speak hopefully that similar words will soon apply to their people. We talk about Indigenous peoples in Canada having their own quiet revolution. Young people are educated in Western schools while also benefitting from the resurgence of Indigenous knowledge. Indigenous writers are proficient in the English language, becoming bestselling and award-winning authors, and Indigenous languages are being revived. My granddaughter is thriving in the SENĆOŦEN immersion program, where she learns to drum and sing and do mathematics and science. Record numbers of Indigenous leaders are serving in federal, provincial and municipal governments, while elected and hereditary chiefs and council members take part in critical economic and resource decision making. Indigenous athletes are winning spots on national and professional teams, and traditional sports like war canoe racing are experiencing a revival. A growing number of Indigenous students are graduating with law degrees, with many of them writing Indigenous law and working on ways to establish Indigenous legal systems.

My children are working toward the day when Indigenous people in Canada tell a story like the one we heard from the young man in the café in Quebec City. No one knows for sure when it will happen, but I think . . . soon.

Thousands of Sweaters

IN 1978 I EMIGRATED WITH my parents from India. I was a young woman, and we lived with my brother and his family in Vancouver. I couldn't speak a word of English, so there was no job I could do. One Christmas my brother bought us wool—my mother, my sister and me—to make presents. The wool came in big round disks like giant hockey pucks. He gave us patterns. My mother and sister did the knitting. The first year, I was the one who sewed all the pieces together. After that I learned to knit as well. We didn't just make sweaters for the family. We made them for everyone. They placed orders.

My brother started selling our sweaters to stores in Vancouver. He couldn't get enough. He had my cousins and my aunties knitting too. We must have knit hundreds of those Cowichan sweaters. Maybe our family made thousands of sweaters. That is such an important memory of when I lived out West.

THE KIRK HALL

QUEBEC CITY HAD BEEN AT the top of my "don't miss" list, even though no one had requested a workshop there and Diane couldn't find any local knitting shops where the owner spoke English. But I had never been to the city with Tex, and what is a road trip without romance?

Just as I was relishing the thought of a free day or two in my favourite city, Diane got a call from Carla. "Can Sylvia come to our knitting group?" Carla asked. "We all speak English, but there are only a handful of us." Yes. Of course, yes.

I met with six members of the Kirk Hall Knitters in the old town. The Kirk Hall, part of St. Andrew's Presbyterian Church, functions as a Sunday school as well as an arts centre. Just as the workshop got underway, a journalist from the *Chronicle-Telegraph*, one of Quebec City's only English-language newspapers and the oldest paper in the province, showed up. The journalist hadn't intended to knit, but by the time we had shared a few knitting stories, she didn't want to leave. We found her some needles and wool, and, much to her surprise, pretty soon she was knitting.

I felt slightly subversive to be meeting with English speakers in a province where French has been legislated, and at a Protestant church hall in such an obviously Catholic province. The church itself is a bold statement on the complexities of Quebec culture. St. Andrew's is the oldest English-speaking congregation of Scottish origin in

Canada. Presbyterians began meeting at that location in 1759, when General James Wolfe's British army was fighting just up the hill and needed a church in which to gather. St. Andrew's is also the site of the oldest English-language school in Quebec and is, arguably, the most important historical site of the Presbyterian Church in Canada. Once I had heard some of the church's history, I sensed the Kirk Hall's ancient welcome.

The feeling at my workshops in Montreal was modern in comparison. For one thing, we met in a suburban mall. Robyn at Les Lainages du Petit Mouton filled a cafeteria twice with English-speaking knitters. Other than the shop's name, we could have been at any mall in the country. The only women who had trouble with English were from Southeast Asia, and they were still learning French as well.

My time in Quebec raised questions for me about church and state, language and law, cultural tensions and politics. But I was most interested in what the province might indicate about the future. How does a country of immigrants find a way to live peacefully together? This is, of course, not just a Canadian question. Every country must find ways to cope with waves of immigrants fleeing war, famine and persecution, or crossing borders for economic reasons. Does the fact that all Canadians, other than the Indigenous people, arrived fairly recently from elsewhere enhance or strain our empathy for refugees and immigrants?

In Quebec City, warming myself on a bench in front of the Chateau Frontenac, I looked east in the direction of Grosse Île, Canada's Ellis Island. In 1832 the government of Lower Canada set up an immigration depot on the island to contain a cholera outbreak that had been brought across the Atlantic. By the mid-1840s the depot was processing tens of thousands of Irish people who arrived starving, diseased, desperate and hopeful that Canada would help them escape the Great Famine. A typhus epidemic killed more than five thousand, who are buried on the island. The lucky ones were dispersed throughout the Maritimes and Upper and Lower Canada and became labourers, fishers and farmers. The Irish constituted the largest influx of immigrants in Canadian history. Likely one of those arrivals is responsible for my (and possibly your) Irish blood.

The earlier wave of immigrants from Scotland and England didn't accept the Irish at first, but soon all three groups blended into Canadian society. That's how it has worked in this country as wave after wave of immigrants arrives from China, Italy, Portugal, Eastern Europe, India and now the Arab countries. Each new group initially encounters fear and resistance as settled Canadians struggle to integrate unfamiliar cultures. But we are a unique population of mixed bloods, and maybe this, along with our new relationship with the Indigenous peoples, will allow Canada to become an important player in a world that so desperately needs examples of how people from disparate places can get along.

WHAT TO KNIT

THE DAY WE LEFT QUEBEC City, I bundled my sketches, maple-leaf graphs, needles and green, grey and black yarn in a bag and tucked it out of sight in the back of the van.

"You can't do that," Tex said. "You wanted to have your Canadian dress finished by the end of the trip, remember? You were going to wear it in Newfoundland. You've already pulled it out and started again at least three times. You can't quit now."

"That's why you drive and I knit," I said. "If it were the other way around, I would never get us across the country, and you would finish the dress and hate it later. I'm not quitting my dress. I'm just putting it away for now."

I was satisfied with the amount of knitting I had done on our trip so far. I had finished a small Prairie Sea Fusion sweater and five baby hats. Tex was frustrated by the seeming lack of progress on my dress, but I was happy with the way the design was progressing.

"It's getting too warm to knit a woolen dress," I told him. "Besides, Nina's instructions are calling out to me."

Back at Creative Yarns in Scarborough, I had loved the tunic Nina, the owner, was wearing.

"Can I get the pattern?" I asked.

"Sure."

Nina got a pen and a good-sized sticky note. She explained aloud as she wrote: "I used a size 5 mm circular needle and started with two hundred stitches, but you can

163

figure out how many stitches you will need. It's about . . ." She counted the spans—tip of thumb to tip of baby finger on her outstretched hand. "Something like seven across the bottom. The one I'm wearing is probably the right size for you, but you can decide how loosely you want it to fit." She described how she had input a garter stitch block down the side of the tunic. "That's what gives it the slightly uneven hem. The garter stitch section dips down a bit."

Exactly the part I liked.

"You just have to play a bit to get the armholes and neckline you want. You'll figure it out from there."

Nina was my kind of designer. A few guidelines on a sticky note and take it from there. Perfect directions for an intuitive knitter. As backup, Tex took a couple of photos of Nina's tunic with his phone.

I had bought a silver-grey cotton-linen blend for the main body of the tunic, and a deep charcoal just in case I wanted to add a design somewhere. I stuck the sticky note on the dash and got started.

For me, buying wool is like buying food when I'm hungry or clothes in September for when the kids are going back to school. It's a necessity. I don't ask the price or care if I have a little too much of anything. It's getting enough that's important, and getting it right. Someone will always eat the leftovers and wear the hand-me-downs.

Because my knitting mind has a background palette of natural West Coast sheep shades—muted creams, greys and browns to black—picking bright colours is always tricky. Yarn shades like ember, cinnabar, tallow, hayloft, almanac, plume and truffle roll off my tongue like poetry, but what if I want Canadian flag red? Would it be called tomato or raspberry? Or is it closer to pomegranate? There isn't a col-our called simply "red." Red is on a spectrum that starts at orange (there is no orange), gets close to purple (there is no purple) and ends up at brown (there is no brown). That's a metaphor I can't resist in my exploration of Canadian iden-tity with all its nuances.

Nine Months, Nine Sweaters

I KNIT NINE WHITE BUFFALO sweaters while I was pregnant. I knit a sweater for everyone in the family, and then started knitting for friends as well. One sweater got me through morning sickness, another through worries about miscarriage. I was knitting when I felt the first kick. With each sweater I got fatter and fatter. I rested my knitting on my pregnant belly and watched it move as the baby's leg or arm poked at my skin. I knit on those final days when I was so big there was nothing else I could do. My daughter is twenty-four years old now, and I still see some of those sweaters kicking around.

NEW BRUNSWICK

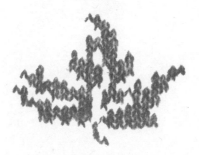

THE OTHER OCEAN

WHILE WE WERE IN QUEBEC City, Tex felt like he was either getting a cold or having an allergic reaction to the spring pollens in the air. Before we left, he took a couple of Benadryl tablets, the first of two road-trip mistakes we made on our way to Fredericton. Half an hour or so out of the city, we had left the farmland behind and were winding our way through endless hills covered in spruce, birch and poplar. Tex's eyes started to droop, and his head began to nod.

He pulled over. "Do you want to drive?"

Unlike the time in Alberta when he had asked me the same question, now he meant it.

"If we are going to get to Fredericton in time for the workshop, we need to keep moving, and I'm falling asleep."

We switched places, and I took the wheel. About three hours later, as we approached Edmundston, New Brunswick, Tex woke up. "If we stop for a coffee at the Tim Hortons up ahead, I'll be okay to drive."

There probably isn't a Tim Hortons on the Trans-Canada Highway that Tex hasn't visited. Luckily for us, this one had a clock on the wall.

"That can't be the right time," I said. "But if it is, we are not going to make it to Fredericton in time for the workshop."

We had crossed over from Pacific Daylight Time to Mountain Daylight Time in Cranbrook, BC, and to Central Standard Time in Saskatchewan. We had changed our watches to Eastern Daylight Time just west of Ignace, Ontario. But we'd forgotten about the next time change.

It was three o'clock, and Google Maps said it would take two hours and forty-five minutes to get from Edmundston to Fredericton. A group of knitters would be waiting at Yarns on York for their workshop, scheduled to begin at 6 p.m. Google's travel estimates were not always right, but because there seemed to be no reliable pattern to its miscalculations, as a rule we believed what it said.

Tex got his coffee to go, and for the first time since we left home he drove five to ten kilometres over his usual personal speed limit. We arrived ten minutes before start time.

Trish had packed the back corner of Yarns on York with twenty people plus a few extras. When Tex and I came swooshing through the front door, dragging our cases and baskets, I drew a deep breath to centre myself. From the din in the back, it sounded like the group was having a party that had been going on for some time.

By the end of the workshop I knew how rock stars must feel on a big tour. "Thank you, folks! I wish I could remember what city I am in."

That night we stayed at a bed and breakfast in an elegant historic house in a residential neighbourhood close to town. After breakfast the next morning we walked down the streets to get a sense of the architecture, the landscape and the people of the city. Later we visited St. Mary's (Wolastoqiyik) First Nation, where Tex had worked. We ate in a trendy downtown restaurant, took a tour of the Legislative Assembly Building and viewed contemporary New Brunswick art at the Beaverbrook Art Gallery.

That evening there was a second sold-out workshop at Yarns on York. This time I really meant it when I said, "Thank you, Fredericton, for inviting us to your wonderful city."

Sheep Manure

WHEN I WAS A KID, we had sheep out behind the house. All they did was stand in one place and stare at us. I thought they were dumb animals. Neither of my parents paid much attention to them. It was a "thing" in those days. Everyone seemed to have sheep. A neighbour guy came around and sheared them. Then a woman from down the street picked up the wool. Dad said he got them because sheep's manure was the best manure for the garden, but he never collected it. So the plops just lay there in mounds until the sheep walked them into the ground.

LANGUAGE

PACKING CLOTHES TO WEAR FOR six weeks in the West, the Prairies, central Canada and the Maritimes, during a cold spring that would become a hot summer, was a challenge. By the time we were in New Brunswick, I needed something summery. We stopped at a mall in Moncton, and I found a dress that would get me through the final days of the trip.

While I stood third in line at the cash, the store clerk and the first customer had a conversation in French.

When the transaction was complete, the clerk passed the bag over the counter and said, "*Salut.*"

Then she turned to the next customer and said, "Hello, how are you this afternoon?"

I was next, and although I gave her no clues about which language I spoke, she greeted me with the same "Hello," without a hint of an accent.

When I finished my purchase, I stood off to one side. I had looked at the woman behind me to see if I could figure out which language she spoke, and also the woman behind her. I couldn't. But the woman at the till knew every time. With no hesitation she switched between English and French, first intuiting the customer's language and then speaking it.

It reminded me of a housing workshop I had facilitated (my real job) in Val-d'Or, Quebec, for a dozen housing managers from the James Bay Cree communities. The organizer, André, who was very French, assured me that my complete lack of French skills would not be a problem. At first I was nervous, then astonished. The participants spoke to me in flawless English. They spoke to each other in Cree, and to André in French. They switched seamlessly from one language to the other in mid-sentence, with gracious generosity.

Now, when I got back into the van in Moncton, I was impressed and hopeful. "Imagine if all Canadians could switch from one language to another," I said to Tex. "Maybe from English to Cree, or Maliseet to French. What if we all learned one other language, not just French and English, but some of us would learn Mandarin, others Hindi or Bengali or Mohawk (Kanien'kéha). Imagine if we could all intuit each other like that young woman did, so that our language transitions would be unbroken."

New Brunswick is the only officially bilingual province in the country, a designation that came after a long and bitter struggle. Acadians settled in the Mi'kmaq and Maliseet territory in the seventeenth and eighteenth centuries. These descendants of French colonists developed a unique, distinctly French language and culture. As the British struggled for dominance of the area in the mid-1700s, they deported thousands of Acadians who refused to pledge allegiance to Britain, sending some to American colonies, some back to Europe and some to the Caribbean. In time, Acadians found their way home to the Maritimes. Given the British hold on Nova Scotia, many settled in New Brunswick.

Maritime society marginalized French speakers until the 1960s, when the New Brunswick legislature passed the Official Languages Act, which made French an official language on par with English. At first the act added fuel to the language controversy, but now, fifty years later, a young cashier can shift from one language to the other as if the barriers of the past had never existed.

The Acadians are finding their rightful place in Canadian society. They are proud of their heritage, but it wasn't until we left New Brunswick and were somewhere in Nova Scotia that I realized the star I saw everywhere, on fences, lampposts and front doors, was a symbol of the Virgin Mary, patron saint of the Acadians. Also known as Stella Maris, "Star of the Sea," this yellow star adorns the red, white and blue Acadian flag seen flying all across the Maritimes.

Home Ec

I WENT TO HIGH SCHOOL in the day when we all took home economics. One of the projects we had to do was to knit a baby sweater. My grandmother had taught me to knit when I was a little girl, so the sweater was no trouble for me. I was done in a couple of days. But the teacher hadn't really taught us how to knit, so some girls didn't have a clue. I offered to knit baby sweaters on an exchange basis. One girl made my apron for me. I also got a lot of math homework done for me that year, and a few science projects.

Knitting Trauma

I HAVEN'T PICKED UP KNITTING needles since the mid-80s. That's when I vowed I would never knit again. I'm here at your workshop because I really liked knitting, and I hope that talking will help me recover my desire to do it.

I chose a complicated sweater pattern from a classy Vogue knitting book. I used what I thought was the best yarn I could find. In those days we didn't think much about the makeup of the yarn, so I don't know what it was.

I could barely understand the instructions. I remember using what seemed like dozens of stitch markers and checking each row off on the pattern one at a time. I made so many mistakes I had to unpick over and over.

It was a long black cardigan that had a poufy collar and poufy bands around the wrists, knit out of some long, hairy novelty yarn. When I finished sewing the pieces together, I put it on. It was a dream sweater with all the '80s sophistication I could muster. It was completely spectacular.

I filled the sink with warm water, exactly like I had read in the blocking instructions.

As soon as the sweater touched the water, I knew something was wrong. My sweater turned into a jellyfish—greasy and slippery, like a body with no skeleton. I pulled it out, and it never seemed to end. My stomach knotted. Panic.

"It will dry back into shape. It has to. Don't overreact," I counselled myself.

I rolled it in a towel and pressed the water out as carefully as possible while chanting prayers to myself.

When I unrolled the towel, the sweater looked two or three times as big as it was before. I laid it flat on a dry towel and scrunched it with my hands to bring it back into shape.

It didn't happen.

I checked every hour or so, hoping for a miracle. Surely the air would suck the water out the yarn, and the sweater would magically return to its pre-blocking shape.

It didn't happen.

I had a terrible realization that my panic was justified. Unscientific as my brain was, I knew enough about air and water to know there would be no miracle. I threw the sweater into a hot dryer.

"I'll shrink it back into shape."

It didn't happen.

The droopy, jellyfish-like masterpiece was dry but had completely forgotten what it was supposed to look like. I felt too sick to put it on. I threw it in the garbage.

It's been thirty years. I need your help to get through that trauma. Just promise me that we will be using real wool, not that synthetic yarn that was all the rage then.

NOVA SCOTIA

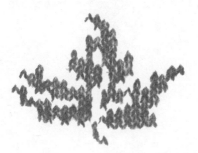

SOUTH NOVA KNITTING TOUR

"IF YOU BELIEVED THE ADVERTISEMENTS about this province, you'd think everyone was an artist. You'd think this was a wooly place," one yarn shop employee in Nova Scotia told us. "It's a promotions shtick. The truth is, Nova Scotia has always been poor, and the idea of a slow, creative life—you know, the eking-out-a-living life—just makes for good press. On the other hand, we have been defined by this bucolic fantasy for so long that I think it is becoming an honest reality."

For years the provincial government has glorified the Nova Scotia "simple life" in order to attract tourists. Some residents see it as a case of cashing in on hard times, of trying to turn the province's weak economy into its strength. Outsiders believe the press. It's the hard-working, hand-working people, the carvers, potters, painters and fabric artists, who give the province the feeling of tranquility and quaintness so sought after by the rushing masses. The ballads and storytelling convince us there can still be meaning in the madness of modern life.

And while Nova Scotians are as up to date as any Canadians, there is also truth to the provincial image of a laid-back, creative lifestyle. As you drive around the southern tip of the province, you will see signs hanging on lampposts or nailed to stakes, advertising an art studio down the driveway. These are old-fashioned invitations to come in, have a cup of tea, stay for a while and, hopefully, buy something.

If I had to recommend the best place in the country for a mini knitting tour, I'd choose southwestern Nova Scotia. You won't need six weeks. Just three or four days, maybe five if you want to take your time.

We started in Halifax at LK Yarns, the city's largest yarn shop, in the historic Hydrostone Market. The heavy cinder-block buildings in the Market, now praised for their charm, were built to give the city a sense of permanence and security after a fire on board a French ship in Halifax Harbour ignited the ship's cargo, causing one of the world's largest human-made explosions prior to World War II when atomic bombs destroyed Hiroshima and Nagasaki. The Halifax explosion, which happened in 1917, killed nearly two thousand people and obliterated almost all structures within an 800-metre radius. The Hydrostone district, once a working-class quarter and now an upscale neighbourhood, is a permanent memorial to the catastrophe that became a defining feature of the city.

Our daytime workshop was held in the basement of a neighbouring building. For the evening workshop, Louise rolled her yarn shelves to the side of her little store so we could fill the middle with knitters. The gatherings were my introduction to how much Nova Scotians love to knit.

If you are doing the South Nova Knitting Tour (I heard the southwest region referred to as South Nova, and I liked how it sounded), you'll want to visit The Loop in downtown Halifax. If you don't know how to knit yet, you could kick off your tour with one of their beginner classes.

"We started teaching beginner classes more than ten years ago," the store manager told me. "I would have thought that by now everyone in the city would know how to knit. But the demand for our classes has never let up."

So it must be true. There are only two kinds of people in Nova Scotia—those who knit and those who want to learn.

Forty-five minutes west of Halifax, you can stop for a coffee at Wool 'n Tart in Wolfville. The tiny shop gives you a hint of the amazing yarns you will find at the owner's main store, Gaspereau Valley Fibres.

If I had to choose the most beautiful yarn store location in the country, Gaspereau Valley Fibres would win hands down. The shop is situated less than ten minutes out of Wolfville in the Annapolis Valley, home to the Apple Blossom Festival and Nova Scotia's best wineries. In the seventeenth century, Acadians built agricultural dykes to salvage the rich farmland from the record-setting high tides in the Bay of Fundy, which would otherwise flood the valley each day.

After wandering Wolfville's charming main street, we headed out of town down a winding road through the bucolic farming country. We dined alfresco on the patio at Luckett Vineyards, overlooking the valley and the bay beyond. When we stopped at our bed and breakfast to pick up the key, a note was tacked on the door of the nineteenth-century farmhouse: *You are the only guests tonight. Make yourself at home. Have a great stay.*

By the time we reached the yarn shop the next day, we were not surprised to find an old farmstead with sheep nodding at the fence and picnic tables next to the barn. We discovered that the store itself was a refurbished auto repair shop built around the oil-change pit. Brenda, the owner, had a particularly good eye for exquisite yarns and exceptional skill at presenting them. It's the sort of place where you aren't sure exactly what is drawing you in, but you know you don't want to leave.

It's hard to overstate the appeal of this wonderful yarn store's location. The agricultural community along the Gaspereau River is home to dairy farms, apple orchards and vineyards made possible by the microclimate in the Gaspereau Valley. The North Mountain protects the valley from the Bay of Fundy on one side, and the South Mountain protects it from the Atlantic Ocean on the other side. As a result, the region conveys a timeless peace and quiet that allows you to believe the press about Nova Scotia: this place truly did seem to offer a simple but fulfilling life.

CONTRARY TO WHAT I HAD expected, the interest in Coast Salish knitting did not diminish as we travelled east. Nova Scotia's knitters brought their old sweaters for my inspection and had lots of questions about the West Coast knitting tradition.

Delia brought a contender for the oldest sweater in the country to one of my workshops at Gaspereau Valley Fibres. My first guess placed the sweater in the 1940s. Delia couldn't say when it was made, because she had bought it at a second-hand store in the early 1960s. It was a buttery cream colour with three bands of simple geometric designs that were now the shade of light milk chocolate. The cuffs were worn thin and frayed in several places, and someone had added a crocheted button band up the front.

"It doesn't look much different today from when I bought it," Delia told me. "It was faded and worn then, just like it is now."

This made me think the sweater couldn't have been knit in the 1940s. That would have made it no more than twenty years old when she bought it. In Cowichan sweater years, that's barely middle age. Cowichans don't look totally faded and worn until much later in life. I speculated that the Gaspereau sweater was knit in the 1930s, making it one of the oldest Cowichan sweaters I'd seen.

TEX AND I DROVE SOUTH along the Bay of Fundy, heading to Shelburne and Studio 138. The place is an art studio, not a yarn shop, but the little town had an enthusiastic group of artists / knitters who squished into a tiny corner of the studio to tell stories and talk about art, design and knitting. Shelburne is one of those "don't miss" towns. Originally a Mi'kmaq village, it followed a common progression, becoming an Acadian settlement, then a Loyalist haven and later a shipyard. Now parts of Shelburne are exquisitely rebuilt and double as historical locations for movies, from Hollywood and elsewhere. The town even played itself in the CBC series based on Lawrence Hill's novel *The Book of Negroes*.

We couldn't miss Yarmouth Wool Shoppe on the town's main street. A sandwich board out front announced Hands on Crafts, which reflected the wide array of products inside. Up front we were met by a mixture of earthy fragrances and a range of woodworking tools and carvings, craft supplies and knitted items. At the back of the store, surrounded by yarn cubbies, was the ubiquitous knitting table, piled with patterns, yarn and unopened boxes. There we met some local knitters who had come out for the afternoon to socialize while they knit.

In the three hours between Shelburne and Halifax, there were six knitting destinations. Becky's Knit and Yarn Shop is in Lockeport, just half an hour outside Shelburne. The little community has 475 year-round residents and only four retail outlets: a market, a gas station/general store, a pharmacy and the yarn shop, which doubles as a hair salon. The shop is a summertime destination, but it's also open year-round, hosting knitting groups and yarn events throughout the winter, as well as the annual Lockie the Lobster Knitting Festival in October.

The Wile Carding Mill Museum is in Bridgewater, an hour north of Lockeport. The mill closed in 1968, after more than a hundred years of service, and is one of only a handful of Nova Scotia's nineteenth-century carding mills left standing. At one time the province had seventy-seven water-powered carding mills. The economic centres of their communities, these mills provided employment for many local women and saved many others a whole lot of work, since the mill's machines could card a week's worth of wool in a single hour.

We took a detour left off Highway 103, driving up Highway 10 for just under thirty minutes, to visit the wool room at Aspen Grove Farm, in New Germany, where raising sheep is the family business. The owners, Jackie and Peter, sell their own yarn as well as local handspun and knitted products. You can visit the shop almost any time if you make an appointment by phone. Otherwise, you take your chances.

Once we were back in Bridgewater, we took Highway 3 east for about twenty-five minutes to the historic town of Lunenburg. During the eighteenth century the Swiss and the Germans helped the British claim the surrounding area for

Protestant settlers. Now the town is a UNESCO World Heritage Site, a model of British colonial town planning that has retained the original layout and many of the wooden buildings. One bright green building in Lunenburg's downtown houses the Mariner's Daughter. The shop sources unique natural fibres and is committed to selling yarns and products from both local farms and international fair-trade suppliers.

"You're on a knitting tour?" people asked us. "Don't miss Have a Yarn. It's one of the best shops in the province."

Have a Yarn is in Mahone Bay. The tiny town, located on the bay of the same name, feels like a place for mariners and boat builders. If I ever make a "best of Nova Scotia" list, Have a Yarn will vie for one of the top spots. The shop has plenty of selection, with a wide range of yarns. It also has an entire wall of sock yarn, so if you are a sock knitter, this is the place for you.

I'm cheating a bit here. Tex and I visited a few of these shops on our Great Canadian Knitting Tour, and some on subsequent trips to Nova Scotia. The rest, which I have visited only by phone, I'll see in person on our next trip to the province. If there is another region in the country with as many wonderful knitting destinations in such close proximity, I don't know about it. South Nova's unique products, open-hearted service and dedication to the knitting craft support the claim that Nova Scotia is indeed a wooly place.

BLACK HISTORY

FEBRUARY IS BLACK HISTORY MONTH in Canada. Every year I make a commitment to learn more about the role Black people played in Canadian history and how Canada's treatment of Black people affected their lives. But on Vancouver Island it's easy to ignore that important part of our nation's story. When we were driving down Highway 103 through Birchtown, Nova Scotia, though, Tex and I came across a plaque that reminded me I needed to live up to my commitment. It read:

> After the American Revolution, over 3,500 free African Americans loyal to the Crown moved to Nova Scotia and New Brunswick where they established the first Black communities in Canada. Birchtown, founded in 1783, was the largest and most influential of these settlements. The population declined in 1792 when many Black Loyalists, frustrated by their treatment in the Maritimes, emigrated to Sierra Leone in West Africa. Although diminished in numbers, Birchtown remains a proud symbol of the struggle by Blacks in the Maritimes and elsewhere for justice and dignity.

Less than ten minutes past Birchtown, in Shelburne, we read about the race riots that had taken place in 1784 between Black and White loyalists who were in a battle for land. Apparently Birchtown had become the largest

Black settlement because it had less desirable land than its neighbour.

Later, online, we found out that by the early 1800s, former American slaves, Black Loyalists and other Black Canadians were leaving Birchtown and settling in Africville, just outside Halifax.

When we returned to Halifax, we visited Africville and found another plaque that read:

> For over a century African Canadians settled here, developing an independent community centred around church and family. As part of the urban renewal project of the 1960s, officials planned to level the community and relocate its residents. The community mobilized, and even though no buildings were saved, Africville became a symbol of the ongoing struggle by African Canadians to defend their culture and their rights. Seaview Park, created on the site as a memorial to Africville, speaks to the enduring significance of community.

Plaques are often the only way busy travellers learn about the sites they visit, but they tell a shiny, sterilized version of the real story. The small, self-sufficient community of Africville did become the centre of Black culture in the Maritimes, but it never received adequate services from Halifax. Drinking water was often contaminated, the city's garbage dump was relocated nearby and a prison was built in the area. Finally, in the 1960s, city officials razed the community, saying they planned to redevelop the area. Even the church was demolished. Many Africville residents believe that the relocation was about racism, not redevelopment, as little development took place in the area. They say the city simply wanted to remove the Black community from within its boundaries.

Our road trip didn't provide enough time for me to pursue my interest in Black history in Canada. But even the limited research I've done since I returned home reminds me that reading plaques is not a good way to discover the real stories. There is so much more I need to learn.

Daddy's Girl

I WAS ALWAYS A DADDY'S girl. I think I took to knitting so easily because I used to sit on my dad's lap while he was mending his lobster traps and netting. He'd give me little things to do when I was really small. The idea of making knots and string into useful things was part of my life from the start. I don't think Dad ever knit. I don't think gender equity has hit knitting yet in these parts. There are plenty of male knitters in the Maritimes, but they are still mostly in the closet. Once in a while, though, I see a man in the yarn store, and he's buying yarn for himself.

CANADA KNITS

FIVE WEEKS ON THE ROAD meeting hundreds of knitters who were all doing interesting projects gave me plenty of time to think about how I fit into the Canadian knitting world. My all-time favourite things to knit are sweaters, vests and skirts. Currently I am also interested in turning sweaters into coats by making them longer, inserting large pockets and fulling the garments to transform stretchy knitting into a more stable fabric. Another one of my current fascinations is felting yarn in the skein. Done right, this process disrupts the fibres and creates something altogether new. Felted single-ply punches way above its weight. It gets elastic and lively, making it perfect for light sweaters and shawls that want to look bulky.

I have also been felting six-strand bulky yarn and making woolen rope. It is great for footstools and floor pillows, and if you use two strands together, you can knit carpets unlike anything I've seen anywhere else.

On the road I met a lot of people who were hesitant to try anything more complicated than a hat or a scarf. "I've been knitting for almost twenty years," one woman told me, "and I've never made a sweater. I'm working up to it. Pretty soon I am going to challenge myself."

I also met the sock-knitting crowd—hundreds of them. I am excited about this field of knitting because I love socks: warm socks, patterned socks, brightly coloured socks, mismatched socks. I haven't knit socks for years, but I know there are many hand-knitted socks in my future.

Most knitters knit for themselves, their families or their friends. Grandchildren are by far the most common recipients of knitted gifts.

Then there are the square knitters, the women who knit squares to be made into blankets for babies, for hospital patients, for the elderly, for shut-ins. Some knitters make squares just to knit; others love the idea of keeping someone warm. These knitters are part of the group of people who knit for a cause. Knitting and politics, knitting and social change go together like a hand and the proverbial mitten. Women have been knitting to change the world since the French Revolution. The *tricoteuses*, immortalized in the character of Madame Defarge in Charles Dickens's *A Tale of Two Cities*, were working-class women who marched to the Palace of Versailles to protest rising food prices. Their outcry forced King Louis XVI to respond. After the Revolution, when the king and other aristocrats were being beheaded, the women gathered around the guillotine, knitting between executions and, according to Dickens, covertly documenting the names of those being beheaded. The women also knit hundreds of conical, red, brimless hats that came to symbolize the French Revolution.

Women on both sides in the two world wars knit socks and sweaters for men, each group hoping the warmth would give their own military the edge. Years ago, an elderly Coast Salish knitter told me that in the 1960s, when First Nations leaders were organizing their resistance to government oppression, knitters paid their way. The meetings of the

National Indian Brotherhood were always held in Ottawa, which meant costly trips for the chiefs from the West Coast. Coast Salish knitters would set up in the crowded waiting rooms of the Vancouver airport with bins of wool and needles, and with toques, socks and sweaters for sale. They knit and sold until they had made enough money to get one of their leaders on the plane. Then they knit and sold some more until they could buy the next chief a ticket.

During the 2017 BC provincial election, my son, Adam, ran as a Green Party candidate. Given the fledgling party's lack of funds, we formed a group of "Green knitters" and sold toques Adam and I had designed for the cause. At first people mocked Adam's fundraising campaign, but pretty soon we were on the front page of the newspaper and were selling as many of the hats as twenty women could produce. The sale of toques became one of his campaign's top contributors, and the other candidates learned that when twenty women gather with a goal in mind and knitting needles in hand, they are formidable opponents. Adam won by a landslide.

The Northern Knitters' baby hats, the Winnipeg knitters' scarfs for people in need, and the shawls, blankets and knitted breastforms for women with mastectomies that are made by other groups across the country are examples of women using their knitting to make intentional, meaningful contributions to society.

On the Great Canadian Knitting Tour, we met knitters who use pins as needles to knit tiny sweaters out of thread, who make wall hangings using yarn and found objects such as seaweed and grasses, and who knit intestines and body parts out of wool for the art of it. We met yarn bombers who knit to lift the spirits of passers-by and to warm trees and bicycles and lampposts. We met technical knitters who are designing complicated patterns with computer programs. They are figuring out knitting algorithms and using terms and techniques I don't understand.

But when all is said and done, most knitters say they knit because they love it. They don't like not knitting.

Look-alikes

I DIDN'T KNOW THE BACKGROUND of the Cowichan sweater until I read your book, *Working with Wool*, but the look-alikes were a craze even back here in the Maritimes. I knit a couple of White Buffalo sweaters for my kids at Christmas, and pretty soon I was getting requests from friends and neighbours. They offered to pay me for knitting. For a few years, while the kids were young, that's all I did. I don't know how many sweaters I knit—it must have been dozens.

PRINCE EDWARD ISLAND

RED, BLUE AND GREEN

I HAVE A CONFESSION TO MAKE. Since I was a young girl I have had Prince Edward Island envy, or maybe it's actually a tinge of resentment. "How come that island gets to be a province and Vancouver Island doesn't?" I would ask myself. It's one of those "it's not fair" sentiments that I've never been able to shake.

It really isn't fair, because Vancouver Island is six times the size of PEI and has five times the population.

PEI got in on the Confederation talks in 1864, with Nova Scotia, New Brunswick and what would become Ontario and Quebec. The place was feisty from the start. Its leaders, men like George Coles and Edward Palmer, said if the Confederation talks didn't take place in Charlottetown, PEI would not attend. They got their way, but then PEI decided it wasn't interested, and it stayed out of the initial union in 1867. The province didn't join the new Canadian Dominion until 1873, two years after British Columbia.

I like that story. In my books, the tiny island's impertinence qualifies it for provincehood. During the same period, however, Vancouver Island was holding down the fort for the Empire and country by keeping the Americans at bay. That should have counted for something.

When Tex and I pulled off the highway to take photos in front of the Welcome to Prince Edward Island sign, I realized that something was wrong. We weren't crossing the usual imaginary line that demarcates one province from another. We were standing on the shore of the Northumberland Strait, a tidal body of water that had been carved out by retreating glacial ice about thirteen thousand years earlier. The illusory line between New Brunswick and Prince Edward Island was somewhere in the middle of the fast-flowing Atlantic waters.

As an island woman, I know what it feels like to go to an island, and this wasn't it. We should have been lining up for a ferry. Tex should have headed off for a cup of coffee and a newspaper, and I should have been pushing back the front seat and pulling out my knitting.

In all my years of ferry waiting, I've never seen evidence of road rage. Where else do you see hundreds of people in cars, with places to go, pull into line and then settle back to wait peacefully? This attitude is unique to island travellers. We like our waits. We turn the supposed inconvenience into an opportunity. I've knit many rounds, sketched many designs and written many stories while hunkered down in my car, waiting for the ferry.

There is the lottery-like element at the ticket wicket when the attendant says, "You might get on the five o'clock sailing, but I'm not sure." There's the anxious anticipation when the line starts moving and the cars ahead of you disappear into the maw of the ferry. But I had no island anticipation as I looked out at one of Canada's top engineering achievements of the twentieth century—the Confederation Bridge. PEI's 12.9-kilometre "fixed link" is the longest bridge in the world to cross waters that become ice-covered in winter. The concrete edifice soars to a height of sixty metres, giving drivers a sensation of flying.

I had planned on driving across the bridge several years earlier, on a previous trip, but was thwarted by a snowstorm.

Given my fear of bridges, I was relieved by the change of plans. But this time I had no choice. We had less than an hour before my workshop was to begin at Julie's Yarn Shoppe in Borden-Carleton, PEI. So, after smiling nervously for a few photos at the welcome sign, I got back in the van.

"Breathe," Tex said as we pulled onto the bridge. "You can't hold your breath the whole way over. It takes about ten minutes."

I gripped the armrest and forced air into my windpipe. It felt more like taking off on a ride at an amusement park than crossing a bridge. Concrete barriers blocked any view of the water, so I was left with an unsettling sense of speed and height, but without the terror caused by looking down.

Tex further calmed my nerves with details. "Did you know they started talking about building a fixed link to the island in the nineteenth century? Did you know that a condition of Confederation was that the federal government maintain a way for passengers and mail to get to PEI? Did you know that every prime minister since Diefenbaker had some sort of plan for a fixed link? Besides this bridge, they considered a floating bridge or a tunnel, like the one under the English Channel. It was finally Prime Minister Brian Mulroney who got the project started, in the late 1980s. Did you know that before the bridge was built, PEI was the only province in the country that had retained its bottling industry? Single-use pop containers were banned."

No. I didn't know anything about the bridge other than its scary qualities. By about seven or eight minutes into the drive I had contained my fear. As long as I kept my eyes on the road and my mind on Tex's flow of incidental bits of information, I was calm.

As the nose of our van tipped toward sea level, I offered a silent thank-you to the engineers who had made the bridge function safely and to the people who had hung in mid-air to build it. Gradually the luscious red island came into view.

The sight was breathtaking. The gentle combination of red ground, green landscape and blue skies was unlike anything I'd seen so far. Apparently Jacques Cartier had the same impression when he first saw the island in 1534. He described it as "the fairest land that may possibly be seen."

Settlement on the island goes back long before the French, English, Irish and Scots arrived. Archaeologists and oral stories place Mi'kmaq communities on the island they called Epekwitk, meaning "to rest on or be cradled by the waves," more than ten thousand years ago. The Mi'kmaq have their own version of Cartier's observation: "If the Creator made any place more beautiful than this, he surely kept it for himself."

FRESH BREAD

LESS THAN FIVE MINUTES FROM the bridge, we saw a sandwich board on the side of the highway that read Julie's Yarn Shoppe. We pulled into the driveway of a quaint nineteenth-century farmhouse.

Julie opened the front door as we stepped up onto the front porch. "Welcome to our island and to our little shop." Her smile and the intoxicating aroma of baking bread were the perfect start to a perfect island experience.

The yarn store was in the living room and hallway of the old house, which was in the process of being renovated to better accommodate the business as well as the family home.

By the time we started, seven knitters had gathered around the dining room table, including Dale, Julie's husband and business partner. Julie served tea and freshly baked squares. Everyone told a sweater story.

Julie had Sheila McGregor's book *Traditional Fair Isle Knitting* awaiting me, along with questions about the connection between Coast Salish colourwork and Fair Isle stranding. She had opened the book to a photo of a scarf with multiple bands of design on each end. Plain-coloured bands of almost the same size separated each design band. The absence of the usual Fair Isle busyness made the scarf look familiar to me.

I had explained the difference between Coast Salish and Fair Isle use of geometric designs the same way in every workshop across the country: "The designs themselves are not significantly different. If you look closely at Fair Isle motifs and isolate them, you will find that many of them are almost identical to the much bigger and easier-to-read Coast Salish designs. The difference is in the negative space. Fair Isle design work leaves no negative space. One motif bleeds into the next, while at the same time the background colours are constantly changing. This blends the horizontal bands together, giving the effect of an overall sea of design. In Coast Salish knitting, bands of geometric design are alternated with plain-coloured bands. It's the plain bands, the negative space, that differentiate the two knitting styles."

Now I was looking at a photo of a scarf with bands of design interspersed with bands of plain colour. It was almost identical to the scarves we knit at Salish Fusion.

Sheila McGregor describes the scarf in her book as an example of early colourwork, dating it back before the beginning of the twentieth century, when stranded knitting first became popular on the Shetland Islands. She describes the less detailed patterning as perhaps the work of inexperienced knitters rather than a design choice.

What she calls unusual, I would call Coast Salish. This was as close as I'd ever come to discovering a bridge between the two styles. On the following page of McGregor's book is a grainy black-and-white photo of a golfer in a Fair Isle pullover similar to the one presented to the Prince of Wales in 1921. The gift is credited with making Fair Isle sweaters popular. What caught my eye on the golfer's sweater were the discrete bands of design separated by bands of plain colour. It looked almost identical to the early Coast Salish sweaters, when it was common for knitters to use many narrow bands of design rather than the three larger bands that later gave the sweater its signature look.

Julie had more questions than I could answer, and by the time I left her shop I thought perhaps I had found the missing link—the places McGregor describes as having had "little idea of how best to apply" designs.

"We've got to go back to Scotland," I said to Tex as we drove toward Charlottetown. "There must be hundreds of these unusual sweaters in people's trunks and in museums that date to a time before Fair Isle looked like Fair Isle and when Scottish knitting looked more Coast Salish." I was suddenly more interested in what the negative space was saying than in what the designs were telling us.

SWEATER COLLECTIONS

"I'LL NEVER BE AS GOOD at knitting as my mother-in-law." The woman speaking was an elegant forty-something who carried herself with an air of accomplishment. "But I'm going to try. Our son is three years old, so I'm already a few years behind."

What she meant was that she had not yet knit her little boy a sweater. Not a turquoise newborn layette, not a six-month hoodie to commemorate his sitting up or a cardigan to mark his first step. She hadn't knit him an alphabet sweater to celebrate his first word or a sailor outfit when he graduated from his first swimming class.

It might sound a bit over-the-top to some, but her mother-in-law had done all that and more for her only son, the husband of the woman at my workshop. The mother-in-law had knit her boy a sweater to mark every occasion in his life until he was fully grown and off to college. She was not only a devoted mother; she knew the value of the collection she had knit. When her first grandson was born, she gave her daughter-in-law all those sweaters. They had been lovingly stored in sealed bags to keep them safe from moths and mildew.

The sweaters now took up the full width of a closet, the woman said. I could imagine their brightly coloured, textured and patterned sleeves in increments of increasing lengths waiting for the next little boy to grow up and, one at a time, wear each of them. The new little boy might not like the slick tunics of the 1970s, the big shoulders of the 1980s or the bright acrylic yarns that were so popular in the past. But his mom was determined that pretty soon she would be knitting her son sweaters in modern shapes and shades, creating a new collection of her own.

WOOLEN MILLS

DURING THE LATE TWENTIETH CENTURY, Canada's wool-processing capability was reduced to a handful of production mills. As a result, even though Canada produces three million pounds of wool a year, almost all of our processed wool has to be imported.

We found Canada's oldest mill still in operation in York Mills, forty-five minutes west of Fredericton, New Brunswick. A woolen mill has been in production in the same location since 1857. The Little family bought the mill in the 1890s and has passed the operations down to the fourth generation. Matthew Briggs bought part of the business in 1916, giving it the name Briggs & Little. Fires forced the mill to rebuild four times: in 1908, 1944, 1956 and 1994. The 1994 fire destroyed the mill building and all the old equipment. Only the offices and storage building were saved.

Although the Briggs & Little machines are relatively new, and their operation looks slick and up to date, they still produce the same Canadian, 100 per cent purewool yarns that, as they say, "your grandma and great grandma used." It was Briggs & Little yarn that made Mary Maxim heavy wool sweaters so durable and so famously Canadian.

The third mill we visited (after Custom Woolen Mills in Alberta and Briggs & Little) was MacAusland's Woolen Mills, in Bloomfield, PEI. It began as a sawmill and gristmill, but it also had a carding machine that turned raw fleece into batts for hand spinning. In 1932 it produced the first version of what would become the world-renowned MacAusland blanket. MacAusland's was forced to upgrade its business in 1949 after a serious fire destroyed all but one piece of equipment. Now the mill has a full operation that includes washing, carding and spinning machines and produces one-, two- and three-ply yarn. But the flagship product is still its MacAusland sixteen-hundred-warp-thread, 100 per cent virgin wool blanket. Following what seems to be a theme in the woolen mill business in Canada, the fourth generation of the MacAusland family is now running the mill.

In Belfast, two hours east of MacAusland's, at the other end of PEI, is a mill with a difference. Belfast Mini Mills processes small batches of local fleece, but the company also specializes in creating small mills to sell, allowing people to process their own fibres. The mini mills are designed to produce limited quantities of top-quality products such as alpaca, llama, mohair, qiviut (muskox) and cashmere. Belfast Mini Mills builds thirty different machines to choose from, which they export around the world.

There was one glaring gap on our road trip: we didn't visit any of the myriad small producers of locally made hand-dyed yarn. In truth, I didn't know where to start. We found many examples of their work in shops across the country. But the gorgeous, mostly variegated yarns are particularly suited to knitting shawls and wraps, something I know very little about. I dream about flowy, funky, flimsy knitted fabric, but I design structured forms. The straight lines and repetition found in geometric designs influence the basic shapes of my finished products. Some of my designs start out being less structured, but by the time I'm finished with them I've pulled in the edges, straightened out the sides and tightened up the borders and cuffs.

While I envy women who wrap themselves in their clothing and appear to dance with their apparel, I don't like it when the things I wear get in my way. The get-it-done side of my personality has me looking for practical clothes. Once I am wearing something, I want it working for me. However, on my next road trip I definitely intend to visit some makers of hand-dyed yarn. Who knows what design dance I will start moving to then?

FINALLY, A FERRY

DURING OUR TIME IN PRINCE Edward Island, we listened to Celtic music during breakfast at our bed and breakfast, drove through fields of potatoes and fallow soil the colour of rusted iron, strolled down Victoria Row, dined in an elegant outdoor café, buried our toes in the warm sand on Cavendish Beach and then made our way to Wood Islands, a tiny farming and fishing community on the southeast end of the island, where we lined up for the ferry to Nova Scotia.

Tex bought a newspaper. I rolled down the window, pushed my seat back and set my knitting on my lap. Cars pulled up behind us. Men got out and leaned against the car hoods. Tex joined them to talk about the weather, the state of PEI's economy and politics.

Although PEI now has box stores and plastic pop bottles, it has not become an ungainly arm of the mainland as I had feared. Some islanders say the construction of the bridge is the most traumatic event in the modern history of the province and that it has challenged islanders' sense of identity. Others still experience PEI as an island bounded by the sea, where the ground is still red and fields are still green. The only thing that has changed for them is that islanders can now come and go as they please.

Vancouver Islanders have been engaged in a similar debate since I was a girl. Would a bridge between the island and the mainland be a good or a bad thing? As I watched

PEI disappear and listened to the hum of the ferry engine, I thought about how long it would take to plan and build such a West Coast bridge, and I was relieved to know it would not happen in my lifetime.

NEWFOUNDLAND

THE ROCK

"SOMEDAY I'M GOING TO SEE Newfoundland." What British Columbian hasn't thought or said that? From rock to rock—there is symmetry in the idea when you live in Victoria. The expanse of our country—the second largest in the world—presents itself as a challenge to be overcome, with the island at the other end your ultimate goal.

By starting our Canadian road trip in Victoria, there was no backtracking or retracing our steps. There was no contrivance to the notion of crossing the country, just the magnetic pull you feel toward the far eastern side when you live on the far western edge of the country.

Yet in spite of both places being islands, I had imagined there would be very little about Newfoundland that would remind me of home. The south end of my island is nestled comfortably in the hook formed by the American Olympic Peninsula and is safe and close to British Columbia's west coast. The Mediterranean climate of the sunny Gulf Islands scattered between Vancouver Island and the mainland gives the area an exotic appeal. The first settlers from the British Isles brought china teacups, silver serving spoons and doilies from their home country, and people still enjoy dainty sandwiches and fancy squares in the afternoon at the Empress hotel. We Victorians tend our flower baskets and take neighbourhood garden strolls on balmy evenings. We like our summers comfortably warm and our winters comfortably cool. When it snows, we close the city down and settle in with a book. There is nothing about Vancouver Island that toughens us up. We are generally a soft and satisfied bunch.

The Scots and Irish and Portuguese who settled the outer rim of the East Coast rock had no such cosseting. I imagined present-day Newfoundlanders would bear traces of the rough-and-ready Viking ancestors who braved North Atlantic icebergs and hurricanes looking for fishing holes. Even the name "Atlantic," from the character Atlas in Greek mythology, conjures images of the Titan who holds the burden of the world on his shoulders. It's a harsh and demanding ocean compared to the Pacific. Western-centred history credits Ferdinand Magellan, a Portuguese naval officer, with "discovering" the planet's largest ocean. As with many such "discoveries," the ocean was first referred to as the "Sea of Magellan." However, Magellan called it Mar Pacifico, now Pacific, meaning "peaceful sea."

The immense land mass that separates our West and East Coast islands raises the question again. What makes Canada a country? What makes British Columbia, the Prairies, Ontario, Quebec, the Maritimes and Newfoundland a political family? Is it that we share common parents? Or at least a common history, with our colonizing British and French believing this massive land was theirs for the taking? Is our commonality found in our Indigenous roots—has the Indigenous connection to their territories kept us grounded, reminding us of something bigger than ourselves? Do we stay together because we are like married people who have been together so long that separation seems impossible? Or are we simply smart, recognizing that divorce is expensive and nobody fully recovers from their financial or emotional losses?

Geographically, it makes sense that a contiguous line of provinces would form a country. At least, it does until you think about the different language and culture of Quebec, the Rocky Mountains separating British Columbia from the rest of the country, and the fact that Newfoundland is a two-hour flight or a six-hour ferry ride from the province closest to it.

Most of us know the general chronology of the birth story of the country called Canada. The country began in the centre in 1867, and by 1870 included Ontario, Quebec, Nova Scotia, New Brunswick, Manitoba and the North-West Territories (renamed Northwest Territories in 1906), expanding the country's reach to the Arctic Ocean. By 1873, British Columbia and PEI had joined the federation, giving Canada claim to the western and eastern shores. In 1898 the Yukon Territory was carved out of the Northwest Territories, and in 1905 the NWT lost more land when Alberta and Saskatchewan became the eighth and ninth provinces. (Canada's last official territory is Nunavut, which joined in 1999.) But it wasn't until 1949, eighty-two years after confederation, that Newfoundland and Labrador voted to become part of Canada. I knew I could not really understand my country until I got to the other side.

I also needed to visit Newfoundland to answer some knitting questions. In my workshops I make the claim that Coast Salish knitting is the only knitting tradition that is truly from North America. "All the other knitting traditions come from somewhere else," I say. In response, I am often asked, "What about Newfoundland knitting? Do you know about their mittens? Don't knitters there have their own knitting tradition?"

For those who don't know already, Newfoundland has an unusual mitten pattern that has been passed down from generation to generation. The mittens are designed to keep three fingers together for warmth, with the index "trigger" finger and thumb separate to allow wearers to have full use of their hands.

Newfoundland knitters will tell you that they also have a signature cap. It's basically a newsboy cap, the classic tam with a small brim. They call it a salt-and-pepper cap.

Some residents of the province claim thrumming as their own too. Thrumming is when you take little wisps of unspun fleece or roving and knit them into your mittens or hat to create a soft, fuzzy lining that is incredibly warm. Although this knitting technique can be traced back to England several hundred years ago, in Canada it is usually associated with Newfoundland and Labrador.

Put these three things together, and some will say Newfoundland can claim a unique knitting tradition. Most knitting historians, however, don't consider these knitting styles different enough from those in other regions to rank Newfoundland knitting in the same category as Fair Isle, Guernsey or Aran, an illustrious group of traditions that encompasses Coast Salish. But while Newfoundland mitts and caps may not be designated an official knitting tradition, there is no doubt that the East Coast knitters are unique, and I had to go there to find out about them for myself.

Art?

I WAS LEAFING THROUGH A magazine at my doctor's office and came across a photo of a sweater by a world-renowned textile designer. It was love at first sight. I had to have that sweater. I didn't care what it cost. I was ready to buy it on the spot. At first I didn't realize it was a knitting pattern, not a sweater, that was for sale.

I was a plain-garter-stitch-scarf sort of knitter, but I didn't let that deter me. Confession: I did something I don't usually do. Really, I don't. I slipped the magazine into my purse and took it home.

I bought the needles and wool—about twenty-five different colours. I can't remember exactly what it ended up costing me, but it was a fortune.

There weren't as many tutorials on the Internet in those days as now, but there were enough to help me get through the pattern. It was a painful process, but I stuck with it. All I could think about was that beautiful sweater and how much I wanted it.

But the closer I got to finishing it, the less I liked it. After about a year, I finished the whole damn thing. I blocked it and laid it out on a towel on the carpet. It was a spectacular work of art, just like the photo that had impressed me that day in the doctor's office. But it wasn't a sweater. At least, it was not something I would ever wear.

When I finally put it on, it looked ghastly. Like something you should put in a vase or hang on your wall, not wear on your back. I hate it. I've never worn it.

NEWFOUNDLAND MYTHS

NEWFOUNDLAND HAS ITS OWN MYTHOLOGY: that it is the most beautiful place on earth; that it has awe-inspiring, rugged landscapes where rough-hewn men and women are forced to forge their survival; that Newfoundlanders have salt water mixed in with their blood, and the rhythm of their daily lives keeps pace with the raging temperament of the Atlantic Ocean.

We'd flown in from Halifax, leaving the van behind. My first impression on the drive in our rental vehicle from the airport to St. John's was that the place was not in any way remarkable. There was rock. Everything was rock, peppered with scrubby pine trees. We passed small suburban developments, malls, gas stations and commercial districts. The sky was grey and cloudy, as it had been during our travels through the Maritimes, and we had no trouble finding CBC on the car radio.

"I don't know what the myths are about," I said to Tex. "This place could be Anywhere, Canada."

Then we crested a hill and the view opened out bit by bit to reveal the city centre, the harbour, Signal Hill, the ocean and the colourful houses I had seen in paintings and photos. Until then I assumed photographers and painters had embellished the yellows and blues and reds. But St. John's doesn't need Photoshop, a sunny sky or even an amber evening glow to be the most colourful city I've ever seen.

The city is perched above a busy working harbour, so the entire population can monitor the comings and goings of the freighters. The garrison on Signal Hill, which was built over the harbour's mouth to defend the colony from European threats, still looks like a gate to the mighty Atlantic Ocean.

It didn't take long for me to feel the magic of this place.

Another myth, one that many Canadians are taught in school, is that the Indigenous people of Newfoundland became extinct in the nineteenth century when Shawnadithit, the last known Beothuk, died.

I had first realized the bleak story was not entirely true when I worked on a housing project with the Miawpukek First Nation. Miawpukek is a thriving, relatively new reserve located at the mouth of the Conne River on the south coast of Newfoundland.

When Newfoundland joined Canada in 1949, the Indian Act did not apply to the new province. This meant First Nations people in Newfoundland and Labrador did not have reserves or Indian status like other First Nations people in Canada. In 1987, after a long struggle for recognition, Miawpukek became the first legal Indian reserve with a land designation in the province.

The struggle for recognition, status and land continues. More than 5 per cent of Newfoundland's population is now recognized as status Indian, and the numbers are increasing. Qalipu First Nation, established in 2011, has joined Miawpukek to become the second recognized First Nation in Newfoundland. As yet, Qalipu First Nation has no reserve land, but it comprises sixty-seven traditional Mi'kmaq communities spread across the province. As of the 2020 government assessment, it has twenty-two thousand members living in the province and elsewhere.

Nowhere in Canada are Indigenous people re-forming society and revising the country's history more than in Newfoundland. The First Nations population in Newfoundland and Labrador is the fastest growing in the country, as record numbers of people are reclaiming their Indigenous roots and reviving their culture.

NONIA

WHEN I WAS STUDYING THE history of Coast Salish knitters for my master's thesis, I was often told about a similar group of knitters in Newfoundland outports whose knitting was an essential part of their survival. It gave me the sense that Canada was bookended by knitting traditions. Not the traditions found in sweaters, mittens or caps but in the hard work of knitters who support their families and communities. Perhaps, I thought, the ties that bind Canada together are yarn and knitters and determination.

I had always wanted to meet the knitters from Newfoundland's famous knitting cooperative. So NONIA, the Newfoundland Outport Nursing and Industrial Association, based in St. John's, was the first place we put on our schedule once we decided on a cross-country knitting road trip, and the last place we planned to visit. NONIA's manager had arranged for one of her staff to take us on a two-day circuit so I could spend time with some of their elderly knitters.

NONIA emerged out of a dark time in Newfoundland's history after World War I. The economy was depressed, there was political instability and the colony lacked even basic services. Most of the province's 263,000 residents lived in one of 1,300 cod fishing settlements scattered along Newfoundland's 9,600-kilometre coastline. These were some of Canada's oldest European settlements. Many had been established by fishermen and whalers and dated back to the sixteenth century.

Medical services were almost non-existent in the tiny outports. So in 1920, Lady Constance Maria Harris (wife of the governor) established the Outport Nursing Committee. With the help of government grants, the committee raised enough money to hire six nurses from England, train them as midwives and open nursing stations along the coast.

The demands of the work were more than most of the English nurses had bargained for, and within a few years both funds and enthusiasm had all but disappeared. However, Lady Elsie Allardyce, wife of Newfoundland's new governor, had heard how women from the Shetland and Faroe Islands, who had knit for the military during the war, continued knitting after the war ended, setting up a cottage industry and marketing their creations. Lady Allardyce was sure that the Outport Nursing Committee could become self-supporting by selling hand-knit garments to pay the salaries of public health nurses.

In 1924, Lady Allardyce restructured the committee and renamed it the Newfoundland Outport Nursing and Industrial Association. Between 1925 and 1934, if a community wanted a nurse, it needed to find five people to form a committee and commit to raising 75 per cent of the nurse's salary. The government paid the other 25 per cent.

People in Newfoundland who wanted their babies born safely, their broken bones set and their old people tended to started to operate knitting businesses. Each outport's volunteer committee ordered yarn and instructions from NONIA's depot in St. John's and distributed them to the knitters. In the early days, NONIA offered knitting classes and canvassed to encourage women to become NONIA suppliers. Most of the proceeds went to funding the nurses, but NONIA also paid knitters a nominal fee. Each local committee was responsible for making sure the knitters were paid and never ran out of yarn.

In 1934 the government assumed responsibility for funding nursing operations on the island. But like wartime knitters on the Shetland and Faroe Islands, once the NONIA knitters had started working, they didn't want to quit. Knitting continued to gain momentum, and NONIA became the central marketer for handwork from the outports. A branch was organized in London, England, and several more were set up in Canadian cities. The demand for NONIA goods grew, and by 1949, when Newfoundland became a province, there were 840 workers in fifty settlements producing NONIA goods.

Today NONIA is a non-profit business run by a volunteer board and a small staff. It employs approximately 175 knitters and weavers across the province, some of whom have been working for NONIA for over fifty years. Their products are in demand by Newfoundlanders, tourists and online customers from around the world.

Before I visited NONIA, I often thought about how much better Coast Salish knitters might have fared if they had not functioned as individual independent producers, each negotiating on her own behalf with the urban merchants. I wondered what would have happened if the West Coast women had formed committees and cooperatively marketed their sweaters. However, I discovered in St. John's that while NONIA had always paid craft workers for their products, it had never offered them a reasonable price. Even though NONIA is run as a not-for-profit, its overhead prevents it from paying knitters more than a token amount. I was disappointed to learn, from my own calculations, that, stitch for stitch, Coast Salish knitters have generally received about five times as much for their work as the knitters in Newfoundland.

WE ARRIVED EARLY FOR OUR appointment at NONIA's shop on Water Street in downtown St. John's. I spent the time browsing through shelves of cable knits, baby sweaters, scarfs, toques, socks and leg warmers. It wasn't hard to look as if I was someone interested in buying. In any store that sells handmade garments, even the most inexperienced salesperson spots me as an easy mark. But nothing jumped out at the NONIA shop that said "buy me." I could feel the fingers of the knitters and hear the clicking of their needles. The quality of the knitting was good but the yarn and colours were dated and the styles looked like Beehive patterns from the 1950s and '60s. I had the sense the knitters were elderly people who had been knitting the same things for decades. I was eager to know more.

In the large upstairs room we met the manager and staff. They appeared to be as interested in our knitting story as I was in theirs. I was excited to finalize plans to tour some of the outports and visit the knitters, and to meet Joanne, our tour guide.

The room reminded me of my own sweater shop from years earlier—a semi-organized wool heaven. Shelves stuffed with yarn, organized by garment type, lined the walls. Piles of socks and sweaters and hats, separated into red, blue, baby pink and yellow stacks, covered the tables. Miscellaneous knitted things overflowed two massive bins, one marked for minor and one for major knitting flaws, that stood next to a working table where employees performed the fixes. When I asked about the bins, one employee told me, "Many of our knitters are getting older, and their eyesight isn't as good as it used to be. It's easier to buy what they have and then fix the problems here."

My management consultant mind slipped into gear. I couldn't help myself. I began making mental notes. Transactions with the NONIA knitters are done through the mail, with no one working face to face on quality control. I picked up a few of the problem garments—button tabs that didn't fit, neck openings that were too big or too small. I wanted to reach for my needles and crochet hook.

I've been called a knitting whisperer, and I realize that is what I am. I spent years in my own shop doing exactly what the NONIA staff were doing: re-sewing pockets, shortening or lengthening sleeves, fastening dropped stitches, you name it. There's not a knitting challenge I'm not excited to solve.

I looked through files of the knitting patterns NONIA had collected over the decades, the organization's beloved old bibles. My guess was that most of the knitters didn't consult the patterns anymore, and some of them had forgotten how to evenly place the buttonholes or attach the sleeves.

As we left the workshop, my heart sank. I had lived this story before. Although NONIA began in a different way than the Coast Salish knitting industry, both became economic schemes for women who otherwise had little or no income. The federal government did not fund either craft movement, but it supported them by way of advertising and promotions. Coast Salish and NONIA knitters produced beloved products that became icons of their respective provinces, but both groups struggled to survive. Knitting is not a contemporary way to make a living, and when the economy of handworkers meets the modern world, the modern world wins.

NONIA is committed to keeping its prices low so that even low-income Newfoundlanders can afford its products. You can get a pair of hand-knit socks at NONIA for only thirty dollars and a pair of trigger mittens for twenty-eight dollars. But low prices also mean the knitters are working for almost nothing.

When I operated Mount Newton Indian Sweaters, in Tsartlip, I struggled to increase the price of Coast Salish knitting so that knitters could be paid a decent amount for their work. However, there are some unavoidable realities in the knitting business. While the value of handwork can be calculated by the hour, it can't be priced that way. Knitting done as art, as one-of-a-kind pieces designed for high-end customers, can be priced to meagrely cover time and materials. Mass-produced handwork has to compete with manufactured clothing for customers who are generally unwilling to pay more for the knitting time. I had not been able to solve that problem, and it appeared NONIA hadn't either.

NEWFOUNDLAND KNITTERS

IT WAS LIKE SAVING THE red Smarties or the juiciest bite for last. I had presented my final workshop in St. John's at Cast On! Cast Off!, an upbeat store with all the latest natural yarns and an enthusiastic crowd of knitters. Tex and I were tired but satisfied. We had seen and done more than I ever imagined we could fit into a single road trip. Now there was just one more thing.

We picked up Joanne early the next morning to get started on the bonus leg of our journey. With limited time available, we were restricted to visiting outports that were no more than a day's drive from the city. We had two days, and she had arranged for us to visit seven elderly NONIA knitters living on the Bay de Verde Peninsula, northwest of St. John's.

When we came across a sign for Dildo, it was the first I'd heard about Newfoundland's love for innuendo.

"Pull over," I said. "Is this a gag? A photo-shoot opportunity for visitors like us?"

There was no pullout beside the road, only a grassy shoulder, but we stopped, and Joanne took a shot of Tex and me with our smiling faces in front of the sign, no doubt like thousands of others before us. I soon learned that Dildo was only one of Newfoundland's strange names for towns. We drove up the road to Heart's Desire and Heart's Delight and could have gone on to Spread Eagle Bay, Ass Rock, Conception Bay and Tickle Cove.

"It must be a cultural thing," I said, "because I don't get it." Surely they couldn't be thinking what I was thinking. I imagined the town hall meeting where the neighbourhood got together to decide on a name for their village—Dildo? Spread Eagle Bay? Did people laugh? Where were the older women, like my mother, who would have put a stop to such suggestions before they got out of hand?

Maybe it was the lack of entertainment in these small places that influenced people's decisions to name their towns after the world's most popular entertainment of all. Perhaps it was an upshot of the long, cold Newfoundland nights. When I asked several of the elderly knitters about the strange names of the towns and if they ever thought about changing the names, they laughed and said, never.

ELDERLY WOMEN MET US AT every stop. They had their hair done, their lipstick on and a cup of tea ready. They had placed samples of their knitting on their coffee tables, and each one of them was ready to tell us her story. One thing we knew for sure when we left Newfoundland was that it is truly one of the friendliest places in the country, and that is no myth.

The women were all seventy-five-years-old-plus, and they had close to four hundred years of knitting experience among them. Some had received gold watches from NONIA for fifty years' service. Most of them didn't knit only for NONIA; they knit for their churches, their families and their neighbours. They loved knitting, but more than that, they could not *not* knit. Stopping knitting would be like stopping living.

NONIA Knitters

IN LESS THAN A MONTH I'll be having my ninety-fourth birthday. I started knitting for NONIA when I was seventeen years old. That's"— she held up her fingers and counted—"seventy-seven years. I got married when I was nineteen and had ten children. I didn't have much time to knit during some of those years, but I started back with NONIA in 1975. That's when I knit my first sweater for them. I like making baby sweaters. I knit for my grandchildren. I've knit for kids across Canada and the United States and England. I've even knit for babies in Cuba. I just love thinking about all those little babies. With NONIA you have to knit what they want. Sometimes I want to knit my own things. I don't really knit for the money. I used to need it more than I do now, but it's a nice little supplement to my pension. We only get a few dollars for each thing we knit. I used to love knitting sweaters with horses on the back, but now I just knit plain sweaters, about one every three or four days. They send me the wool. I like to have wool around. This way I'm never without.

I GOT INTERESTED IN KNITTING when I used to help my aunt wash and card her wool. I remember it from when I was just a little one, seven or eight years old. She was in Fortune Bay. There wasn't very many sheep, but she used all their wool. She didn't waste a thing. I'm more than eighty now. I knit lots of Mary Maxim patterns. Nowadays I like to knit cables. They give us the patterns

231

and say knit #2 or #4, but I've memorized the patterns now, and I don't use them anymore. I don't knit as fast as I used to. It takes four or five weeks now to do a pullover, another week to do a cardigan. We used to meet in the hall in Salmon Cove. The woman from NONIA would be there with boxes of wool. That's where we learned how to knit certain patterns, and then she'd take our knitting back to the Depot and she'd pay us. Now we have to ship our work out, and the cost is high, so sometimes we pool our work together and fill a big box. I remember my grandma knitting while it was dark and knitting while she was reading *Downhome* magazine. I hope I can keep knitting and sending them my sweaters. Now I'm living in this old people's home. It's good here as long as I get my box of wool in the mail, as long as I always have something to knit. I couldn't afford to keep myself supplied with wool otherwise.

I STARTED KNITTING WHEN I was about sixteen. That was over sixty years ago. Everyone still knows how to knit, but most don't do it anymore. My mom taught me, but it was my grandma who showed me how to turn a heel. Mostly I like knitting socks and caps. I like knitting in the morning and the evening. I like knitting in the car. Actually, I like knitting all the time. The only time I'm not knitting is when I'm playing cards or at bingo. I knit shawls for church fundraisers. I sell some to shops who resell them, and one time my granddaughter put some of my pieces online and sold them for me. At Christmas, NONIA gives us a bonus, but we haven't had a pay raise in years. There's no way I'm doing this for the money. But they keep me in yarn, and I always like to have yarn around the house and an order to make.

YOU ARE GOING TO MEET two of us. My sister and I are from Hant's Harbour, and we both love to knit. My mother knit for NONIA for fifty-six years. She was a really fussy knitter. Her work was perfect. After she'd been working for them for fifty years, they presented her with a gold watch. I worked for thirty-three years in a crab plant, but I still knit even then. In those days there was a knitting centre in the village, and a woman came around and brought in wool. She gave it out to all of us knitters along with patterns and instructions. They even gave us knitting classes. I like making hats and scarfs and mittens. I have made hundreds, maybe a thousand, salt-and-pepper caps. They don't come around anymore and teach people how to knit. I hope that NONIA stays in business and that my hands and eyes stay good so I can keep working. Every time I sit down I pick up my knitting. There's just me and my sister now . . . we don't have anyone to pass it on to.

I'VE KNIT FOR NONIA FOR twenty-five years. They had a big do at the governor's house where they invited all the knitters. They talked about how we're part of Newfoundland's culture. Who'd have thought? I used to just knit for my kids. I had seven of them. But then when my husband died I needed extra money. I saw an ad in the newspaper, and I sent away to the address and got back a box of wool in the mail. I used to just knit baby sets for them. I didn't get paid much, but it was something I could do at home. Now I just knit for fun. It's no good to just sit. I got to do something with my hands. Now cable sweaters are my specialty. I like to do the cardigans. They take me three weeks. I have my card games at the seniors' centre and church. Otherwise I'm knitting. So I'm busy, oh, pretty much all of the time. I make special orders, and I always sew in an extra button.

GOING HOME

I'D SUGGESTED WE SELL THE van in Halifax. I would have been willing to give it away. The van had worked hard for us, and surely it was at the end of its life. I was at the end of my journey, and getting home was the only thing I had in mind. Tex, on the other hand, had work to do in Huntsville, Ontario, and belongings he wanted to move out west. So the poor old red van had one more cross-country trip to make and, almost inconceivably, Tex was looking forward to the return drive.

"It'll be so much quicker going back," he enthused.

"There is no possible way that driving 6,200 kilometres can be considered quick."

"No workshops. No yarn stores. No knitting destinations."

I could see his point.

At the airport in St. John's, after giving me an exhausted kiss goodbye, Tex caught a flight to Halifax, where he picked up the van. As it turned out, the drive home took him only six days. I flew from St. John's to Vancouver, with stopovers in Montreal and Toronto. Just under thirteen hours after our goodbye kiss, I landed at the Victoria airport, a five-minute drive from home.

On an early leg of the trip I sat next to a woman from Sarnia. She had been in St. John's to meet her newborn granddaughter. The woman hadn't had a good night's sleep in two weeks. Her daughter was breast-feeding the baby, but it wasn't going very well. The baby appeared to be always hungry. "I would have given her a bottle," she said. "But you know how it is. You can't say too much. What were you doing in Newfoundland?"

I could have told her that I had been on a search for what it means to be Canadian, that I had been looking for my people and that my mission had been to find out what knitting and knitters could tell me about Canadian identity. I could have said that my unfinished green-maple-leaf dress was stuffed in the bottom of a box. I thought about telling her that I had finally put all the puzzle pieces together, that I now knew how to make the design for my Canada dress work.

But she looked tired, and I didn't have enough energy to explain myself.

I think I said something like, "I taught a knitting workshop in a lovely little yarn store in St. John's."

"My, that's a long way to come for a workshop."

"Yes," I said. And then we both fell asleep.

LAST THOUGHTS

I HAD LEFT VICTORIA AN ambivalent Canadian, conflicted about my country's colonial past while at the same time thankful for my abundant life. I came home a hopeful Canadian. Our knitting road trip didn't offer any definitive answers to the question I set out with: "What is a Canadian?" But the land and the people we met gave me inspiration, and I returned with a different perspective. In the end, it was through writing this book that I gained a new understanding of my country and discovered a side to my Canadian self I hadn't known before.

If knitters represent what it is to be Canadian, then we are a country of hard-working, caring, creative people leading meaningful lives. We are interested in who we are and where we come from. We are intentional and brave, ready to hear the tough stories of our past and use them to forge a new future. I am old now, and not so naïve as to believe that all Canadians, or even all Canadian knitters, are like the ones I met, but I wish they were.

My children are W̱SÁNEĆ people from Tsartlip First Nation. The original name for their village is JSIN̲SET meaning something like "the people who are growing themselves up." JSIN̲SET is a fitting word to use for Canada. We are no longer an adolescent country, stuck in the fantasy of our youth. Some of us may still miss our childhood, the days when we believed we were always the good guys. But most of us want a more genuine sense of our country, one that will come only from listening to the real stories of our past, the light and the dark. Canadians are writing new stories about their country, stories that not only illuminate the destructive colonial past but also present a different and more sustainable, Indigenous way to think about land and resources, and that celebrate the re-emergence of Indigenous culture and languages. If my premise that Canada cannot be whole, cannot be mature and cannot have a true identity until it comes to terms with its colonial past and its Indigenous present is accurate, then the Great Canadian Knitting Tour gave me reason for optimism. Canada is growing itself up.

The land and people that make up Canada defy the pigeonholes of a travel book, and so they should. In 1971 Prime Minister Pierre Elliott Trudeau told the Ukrainian-Canadian Congress, "There is no such thing as a model or ideal Canadian. What could be more absurd than the concept of an 'all-Canadian' boy or girl? A society which emphasizes uniformity is one which creates intolerance and hate." The Canada I encountered is a country of diversity and tolerance.

The physical attributes of each region are starkly different—the imposing western mountains, the undulating foothills of the Prairies, the Ontario lakes that look and feel like oceans, the bucolic farmland of Quebec, the dignified Maritimes and the giant rock of Newfoundland. The knitters of Canada are as diverse as their country's geography. But their textured and colourful stories about knitting create a common narrative. The stories I heard were about knitting as a political act, as an act of caring for others, as an expression of hope and promise. For some, knitting was a way to relieve stress; for others, a recovery strategy. Knitters' stories were about creative expression, about family ties and history, about knitting as a social act. Some women told stories about knitting for a living. Knitting, it seems, is a vehicle for all kinds of stories about everyday sorts of things.

I also learned during my travels about the unique role yarn shops play in Canadian communities. There were common threads that knit the shops together. They were all owned by women. They all had a group of committed customers. The shops turned knitting into a social event. The owners were all, to some degree, artists who were broadening the idea of knitting to encompass new materials, new shapes and new tools.

There is nothing more Canadian than small business. There are 1.1 million small businesses in Canada, and more than half of them have fewer than five employees. While yarn shops face the same challenges and reap the same rewards as other small struggling businesses, something else is going on. These businesses are not philanthropic. They are not charities. The owners are passionate businesswomen, smart and savvy. They know how to buy, sell, budget and promote. However, the transactions in these shops are not simply, or even primarily, exchanges of product for money. In these stores, success is calculated on multiple bottom lines that include artistic expression, education, cultural sharing and developing and supporting community. Human satisfaction is more than a sales pitch; it's the key ingredient. Perhaps it's the female factor that makes yarn shops examples of capitalism done differently, places where humanity leads, not the dollar. Similarly, I met mill owners who operate their companies with bottom lines that incorporate their determination to use Canadian wool, to adopt environmentally sustainable practices and, most importantly, to keep age-old traditions alive.

One goal of my cross-country knitting tour was to share my experience of living and working with Coast Salish knitters. Their stories encompass poverty, discrimination, hard work, innovation, industriousness, love, family ties and racism. These were women who made their lives work in spite of the country they lived in, not because of it. What better archetype for colonization in Canada than the Cowichan sweater?

Along the way, I discovered that knitters everywhere share many rich characteristics with Coast Salish knitters. They are keen to learn, sensible, lovers of beauty, caring and productive people. They use every brand of yarn, but hand-dyed or undyed natural fibres are often their first choices. There is a large group of scarf and shawl knitters, a committed contingent of sock knitters, knitters who make only "small stuff" and those who knit anything and everything. They all came to my workshops to challenge themselves and to expand their knitting horizons. I heard profound stories from the knitters I met, as well as simple memories. They were all told in the same rhythm that Ella, my five-year-old granddaughter, falls into as she sits on my lap with her needles and yarn: "Put the tip in, wrap the wool around, pull it through and push it off. Put the tip in, wrap the wool . . ." One evening not long ago, Silas, Ella's ten-year-old brother, was sitting in our living room along with my local knitting group. As he concentrated quietly on making a toque, he said, "This is so peaceful." He was right.

When I asked the knitters I met what symbolized Canadian knitting for them, overwhelmingly the answer was a bulky cardigan with motifs on it. That sweater has many names and variations. Not everyone wants to wear one, nor is everyone fond of the look of them. But everyone loved those sweaters nonetheless and identified them as truly ours. The road trip is over, but the journey continues. My half-finished green-maple-leaf dress is bundled in a drawer, but I am ready to knit the rest of it now. I'm still not a flag-waver, but I will wear that dress with a new respect and love for this magnificent land.

ACKNOWLEDGEMENTS

BEFORE I THANK THE PEOPLE who helped create this book I must acknowledge the land and waters of the places I travelled. For the coastlines, mountains, prairies and forests, for the lakes and rivers, and for the wild creatures that inhabit the natural world in which humans reside I am in awesome wonder and filled with deep gratitude. I also acknowledge the timelessness of this environment and the brief speck of time in which I make my observations and write my stories. And now, I want to take a few moments to acknowledge the Indigenous peoples who have lived in these lands since habitation was possible. I acknowledge the human struggle for survival and for meaningful existence that defines the country we call Canada.

Thank you to Laura Olsen, my late mother-in-law. "Come over here," she would say when I visited her. Then she'd examine the knitted skirt or sweater or vest I was wearing. "Let me look at that. How did you do that? Where did you find that design?" We shared our techniques and our love for making wool, knitting and geometric designs. Laura, I thank you now and forever for your generosity of spirit. And just a note: I still use your knitting needles.

The tour: this book began with an idea for a road trip to promote my 2015 book of essays and knitting patterns, *Knitting Stories*. Thank you to Diane Morriss and Sono Nis Press for helping me grow the idea into the full-fledged cross-country knitting tour it became. Thank you, Diane, for doing everything from connecting us to knitting shops and craft guilds, to organizing dates and times for workshops, to sharing your audio books so we had good stories on the road.

I'm sending a big hug to Joni Olsen, my oldest daughter and knitting partner. Joni made the kits—more than nine hundred of them—for the participants in the workshops.

Thank you to all the forty-odd shop owners and managers who generously opened your stores and hosted workshops, and to the hundreds of participants who eagerly came to learn new knitting techniques. Deep thanks especially to the knitters for sharing stories from your heart and making the tour profoundly moving for everyone involved. I hope I have represented all your thoughts and feelings in the stories I have included in this book.

There never would have been a knitting tour without my incredible husband, Tex. He made it happen; it's as simple as that. I cannot imagine there is a better tour guide in Canada than Tex. From the red rock in the Canadian Shield near Thunder Bay, to the importance of the little town of Sioux Lookout, to the history of the Confederation Bridge in PEI, Tex has stories you won't find anywhere, not even in Wikipedia. Thank you, thank you, thank you, my love, for opening my eyes to things I had never imagined and for making the trip stimulating and fun.

The book: many months after we got home Tex found his notebook and began reading the stories to me that he had recorded in the workshops. We decided the tour itself was a story and so this book was hatched. Thank you, Sono Nis, for working with me to get the book started. Thank you, Barbara Pulling, for the initial edit. A special thanks to Audrey McClellan who stuck with me for several passes, pushing and pulling my work into places I would not have gone on my own.

COVID-19 hit *Unravelling Canada* hard. Tex and I came down with the virus early on and it stuck with us for an unusually long time. So when Sono Nis Press decided to suspend its publishing activities I was left with a nearly completed book that I was prepared to give up. Tex prodded me to stick with it, and thanks to the help of Adam, my son, I connected with Anna Comfort O'Keeffe at Douglas & McIntyre. Her offer to publish brought the book back to life. I have extreme gratitude for Anna and the team at Douglas & McIntyre who believed in the book right away. Especially to Rebecca Pruitt MacKenney who took it on, thank you, thank you, thank you, Rebecca, for your fresh eyes and your rigorous edits. It was a privilege working with you.

And now I circle back to Tex. This book is our story, not mine. Tex didn't only encourage me to write it, he listened to every idea I had, he heard every iteration of every chapter, paragraph and sentence. He added his memories to mine and reshaped some I had half forgotten. He edited and then edited again until we decided the book was finished. Tex was as important to this book getting done as I was. Again and again, thank you, my love.